VERY MERRY

COOKIE PARTY

A GIFT FOR: _Lisa_

FROM: _Mom Ruth_

VERY MERRY

COOKIE PARTY

How to Plan and Host
a Christmas Cookie Exchange

BY BARBARA GRUNES & VIRGINIA VAN VYNCKT

PHOTOGRAPHS BY FRANCE RUFFENACH

Hallmark

GIFT BOOKS

CHRONICLE BOOKS

SAN FRANCISCO

THIS EDITION PUBLISHED IN 2011 BY HALLMARK GIFT
BOOKS,
A DIVISION OF HALLMARK CARDS, INC., UNDER
LICENSE FROM CHRONICLE BOOKS,
KANSAS CITY, MO 64141
VISIT US ON THE WEB AT WWW.HALLMARK.COM.

DESIGNED BY SARA SCHNEIDER
FOOD STYLING BY ELIZABETH DER NEDERLANDEN
TYPESETTING BY JANIS REED

ISBN: 978-1-59530-426-1
XKT4001

PRINTED AND BOUND IN CHINA

Acknowledgments and Dedications

FROM BARBARA

To my husband, Jerry Grunes, and to my daughter, Dorothy Grunes, cookie taster extraordinaire, for their endless encouragement.

To my grandchildren, Marissa, Avi, Claire, Big Natalie, Suzie, Big Noah, Ethan, Natalie, and Noah.

And to cherished family and friends, for their tasting and support: Abel Friedman, our sugar consultant, and his lovely wife, Judy.

FROM VIRGINIA

To my husband, Marv, and my children, Lian and Daniel, for tasting and offering their honest and valuable opinions on the cookie recipes, successful and otherwise. And to my parents, Fran and John Van Vynckt, and my brothers and sisters, Randall, Ray, Ron, Viv, and Vicki, for enduring all those baking experiments so many years ago.

CONTENTS

INTRODUCTION 9

PART 1: PLANNING AND HOSTING
A COOKIE EXCHANGE 11
   Cookie Exchange "Rules" 12
   How to Make Your Cookies Look Their Best 13
   Presentation and Packaging 20
   Party Themes 20
   Party Menus 21
   About the Recipes 30

PART 2: COOKIES TO BUILD A PARTY AROUND 33
   Chapter 1: Dear Santa: Dressed-Up Classics 34
   Chapter 2: Ginger and Spice 48
   Chapter 3: For Chocoholics 60
   Chapter 4: Cookie Ornaments 78

PART 3: COOKIES BY TECHNIQUE 101
   Chapter 1: Drop Cookies 102
   Chapter 2: Bars and Squares 126
   Chapter 3: Rolled and Cutout Cookies 148
   Chapter 4: Slice-and-Bake Cookies 164
   Chapter 5: Filled Cookies 180
   Chapter 6: Molded and Stamped Cookies 204
   Chapter 7: Pressed and Piped Cookies 232

SOURCES 240
INDEX 241
TABLE OF EQUIVALENTS 247

INTRODUCTION

Bless the baker who first thought up the cookie exchange. In the madness of the holiday season, who wants to make dozens of different kinds of cookies? Yet, Christmas wouldn't be nearly as much fun without a seemingly endless assortment of cookies, especially nicely decorated ones.

So, some friends decide that each one of them will make one type of cookie. Then, they'll get together and everyone will exchange what they have made. You arrive with, say, six dozen butter cookies—one dozen for the party and one dozen for each of the other partygoers—and you leave with a dozen each of chocolate chip cookies, biscotti, shortbread wedges, candied cherry slices, toffee squares, or other treats. It's a truly inspired way to share the baking burden of the holidays.

Cookie exchanges can range from folks bringing a couple dozen cookies to share with colleagues at work to a tree-trimming party with a full menu, elaborate presentations, and games and prizes. Put together the kind of get-together you are comfortable hosting, keeping in mind this is the holiday season. In other words, make sure to have fun with it.

If you're attending a cookie exchange hosted by someone else, remember that it will be a chance to show off your baking skills and to give another family the pleasure of tasting some of the best cookies ever. The recipes in this book can help you achieve that.

PART 1

PLANNING AND HOSTING
A COOKIE EXCHANGE

If you're hosting the cookie exchange, it is up to you to coordinate the baking efforts of your guests. In other words, you need to make sure each of your guests is bringing a different kind of cookie. You will also need to decide the "theme" of the guest list. For example, do you want to invite the most experienced cookie makers you know to show off their best creations? Or, do you want to ask colleagues from work? Your family's legendary cookie bakers? Friends who love chocolate?

Once you host your first cookie exchange, you'll find that it can quickly become a tradition. If the same guests attend the get-together every year, consider rotating the hosting duties to share the work.

People are typically busy during the holiday season, so the further ahead you can schedule the party, the better. Proper etiquette calls for printed and mailed invitations. But let's face it, we live in the digital age, so a postage stamp is not the only way to bring people together. However you decide to get the word out, be sure to make the invitations fun. All sorts of free or inexpensive royalty-free clip art and photos are available on the Web that you can use for making eye-catching invitations.

If you decide on e-mail invitations, ask the recipients to acknowledge receipt, whether they plan to come or not. We know from experience how embarrassing it feels to learn from a good friend that she never saw the invitation because her computer was down or our message was shunted into her junk e-mail folder.

COOKIE EXCHANGE "RULES"

Exchanges vary according to how rigorous the "rules"—actually, they're more like guidelines—are. We have found that people who have been hosting cookie exchanges for years tend to be a bit stricter than those who are new to the tradition.

Some exchanges ban everyday cookies such as chocolate chip or oatmeal, but we see no reason to do this, as long as you make sure everyone doesn't bring chocolate chip cookies. Also, encourage the partygoers to dress up the classics: Add some dried cranberries to the oatmeal cookies, rim the edges of chocolate chip cookies with chocolate, make marbled or layered brownies.

Some exchanges forbid no-bake cookies, on the grounds that they're too easy to make and/or aren't as tasty as their baked counterparts. Again, we see no reason to exclude them, as long as people try to make them as celebratory as possible. Not everyone is a world-champion baker, and even a beginner can dress up the old cereal treats for a party.

We think it works best to have as few rules as possible, especially if this is the first time you are hosting an exchange or your guests vary widely in their baking abilities. Here are three guidelines we strongly recommend:

1. Cookies must be homemade. After all, the opportunity for people to show off their baking skills and share their creations with others is what a cookie exchange is all about. Make exceptions for emergencies. If on the afternoon of the party, Sadie's dog knocks five dozen cookies onto the floor and eats half of them, it's too much to expect Sadie to make five dozen new cookies. Sadie can visit a good bakery and select some pretty cookies to bring and share—assuming she has any money left after the vet visit.

   If you're a group of people who love to eat cookies but not necessarily bake them, you can always allow everyone to use store-bought dough and dress up the cookies with decorations.

2. Each participant must bring the requested number of cookies. That's only fair. If for some reason, a partygoer can't bring that amount, then that guest will take home fewer cookies. The exception would be if someone brought oversized ornamental cookies, such as gingerbread people, that would earn several smaller cookies, such as spritz wreaths. Decide in advance how the cookie "currency" will add up.

   How many cookies should each person tote home? That depends on the size of the guest list. If there are only four or five of you, it's reasonable to ask that everyone bring five to six dozen cookies. If the gathering numbers twenty, it's not realistic to expect someone to bring two hundred plus cookies. In that case, each person might get three of each cookie.

3. Ever go to a party and see someone wearing the same dress you're wearing—except that she looks ten times better in it? You can get the same sinking feeling if you bring shortbread made from your grandmother's beloved recipe, only to discover that everyone is raving about someone else's shortbread. That is one reason

cookie exchange invitees must let the hostess know in advance what kind of cookies they plan to bring. Another reason is variety. Russian tea cakes or chocolate chip cookies are delightful, but not if eight people show up with them.

HOW TO MAKE YOUR COOKIES LOOK THEIR BEST

The cookies you contribute to a cookie exchange will be going home with others, so making your batch appealing is important. You can dress up such classics as chocolate chip or oatmeal by mixing in higher-end ingredients, shaping them differently, or adding decorative touches, such as a chocolate dip or colored decorating sugar. In Dear Santa: Dressed-Up Classics (page 34), you'll find ideas for lifting everyday cookies out of the ordinary.

Here are some ideas for decorating your cookies in grand style, using techniques, icings, and decorating ingredients guaranteed to make your baking efforts shine.

PIPING

Piping icing onto a cookie is the easiest way to give it a polished, professional-bakery look. For fine work, use Royal Icing (page 14). For larger decorations, use buttercream or a similar icing in a pastry bag fitted with the tip of your choice. Three standard tips—open star, round, and leaf—can take care of just about any cookie-decorating job. Disposable pastry bags save you cleanup time, and plastic couplers make changing tips in mid-decoration easy.

Ready-made decorator icings in tubes simplify life for the cookie decorator. Small tubes of icing (usually gel) with narrow tips are ideal for writing or outlining. Larger tubes of opaque icing require plastic decorating tips (usually sold separately) that screw onto the end of the tube. Cake Mate and Wilton are two popular brands. At cool room temperature, these icings can sometimes be a bit hard to squeeze. Put the tube in a glass of hot water briefly to thin the icing so it will pipe more easily.

ICINGS AND BUTTERCREAMS

For a smooth satin finish that you can paint or color, use Poured Fondant Icing (page 15) or Easy Vanilla Icing (page 16). Royal Icing dries hard and typically works better for detail work than as an all-over cookie coating. Buttercream (page 17) tastes better than other cookie icings but stays soft, so cookies iced in buttercream must be stored in a single layer. Buttercream also makes an excellent filling for sandwich cookies. If you are decorating with colored sugars, add them when the icing is still damp so the sugar will stick. If you are decorating with food coloring or with a second icing of a second color, let the base icing dry completely first.

ROYAL ICING

makes about
1 1/2
cups

This is the "glue" that holds gingerbread houses together and makes it possible to pipe fine designs in relief. Once it is dry, it is hard and virtually indestructible. Using pasteurized or dried egg whites eliminates the small risk of salmonella from raw eggs.

2 PASTEURIZED EGG WHITES OR RECONSTITUTED DRIED EGG WHITES

¼ TEASPOON CREAM OF TARTAR

2½ CUPS CONFECTIONERS' SUGAR, OR AS NEEDED

1 In a bowl, with an electric mixer, beat together the egg whites and cream of tartar on medium-high speed until soft peaks form. Gradually add the confectioners' sugar, beating until a thick, glossy icing forms. On high speed, beat until the icing stands in stiff peaks, 3 to 5 minutes. If the icing is too soft, beat in additional confectioners' sugar, a tablespoon at a time. If it is too stiff, beat in water, a teaspoon at a time.

2 Use immediately, or cover tightly and store at room temperature for up to 2 days. (Do not refrigerate.) It will become spongy during storage, so beat again briefly with an electric mixer on medium speed before using.

POURED
FONDANT ICING

makes about
2/3
cup

This icing sets to a smooth, dry finish, making it ideal for decorating cookies as is, or for tinting with food coloring for making painted cookies.

1½ CUPS SIFTED CONFECTIONERS'
SUGAR, OR AS NEEDED

1 TABLESPOON MILK

¼ TEASPOON LEMON, ORANGE,
OR VANILLA EXTRACT

3 TO 5 TEASPOONS LIGHT CORN
SYRUP

1   In a small bowl, whisk together the sugar, milk, and lemon extract. Stir in 3 teaspoons corn syrup. The icing should be just thin enough to pour, but not so thin that it will run over the edge of the cookie. If the icing is too thick, thin it with additional corn syrup, adding 1 teaspoon at a time. If it is too thin, add additional confectioners' sugar, 1 teaspoon at a time.

2   Use immediately, or cover tightly and store at room temperature for up to 2 days. (Do not refrigerate.) Whisk or beat briefly before using.

CHOCOLATE POURED FONDANT ICING

Substitute 3 tablespoons unsweetened cocoa powder for ¼ cup of the confectioners' sugar, and use chocolate or vanilla extract in place of the lemon extract. Proceed as directed.

VANILLA ICING

makes about
1½
cups

Similar to fondant, this icing sets with a smooth finish. If you are not using a food processor, sift the sugar to avoid lumps in the finished icing.

2 CUPS CONFECTIONERS' SUGAR

1 TEASPOON VANILLA EXTRACT

4 TO 6 TABLESPOONS HEAVY CREAM OR MILK, OR AS NEEDED

FOOD COLORING OF CHOICE (OPTIONAL)

1 To make the icing in a food processor, combine the sugar and vanilla in the processor bowl. With the machine running, pour the cream through the feed tube, adding just enough cream to form a smooth, spreadable icing.

To make the icing by hand, sift the confectioners' sugar into a bowl. Add the vanilla, then whisk in enough cream to make a smooth, spreadable icing.

2 To tint the icing lightly, add a drop or two of food coloring and whisk to color uniformly. Use immediately, or cover tightly and store at room temperature for up to 2 days. (Do not refrigerate.) Whisk briefly before using.

makes about
1 1/2
cups

CHOCOLATE
BUTTERCREAM

For a tangy counterpoint to the sweetness, substitute sour cream or buttermilk for the milk. Use unsweetened dark cocoa powder (see page 66) for a deep brown, almost black icing.

6 TABLESPOONS (¾ STICK) UNSALTED BUTTER, AT ROOM TEMPERATURE

3 TABLESPOONS UNSWEETENED COCOA POWDER

2 CUPS CONFECTIONERS' SUGAR

1 TEASPOON VANILLA EXTRACT

2 TO 4 TABLESPOONS MILK OR HEAVY CREAM

1   In a large bowl, with an electric mixer, beat together the butter, cocoa powder, sugar, vanilla, and 2 tablespoons milk on low speed until the confectioners' sugar is incorporated. Increase the speed to medium and beat for 2 minutes until a smooth, spreadable icing forms. If the icing is too thick, beat in additional milk, a teaspoon or two at a time.

2   Use immediately, or cover tightly and refrigerate for up to 2 days. When ready to use, let stand at room temperature until easily spreadable.

VANILLA BUTTERCREAM

Substitute ¼ cup confectioners' sugar for the 3 tablespoons cocoa powder and proceed as directed.

STENCILING

Cookie stencils, available in crafts stores, make it easy to imprint a design in decorating sugar or icing on a cookie. You can also make your own stencils by cutting a simple design out of cardboard or acetate. Flat cookies are easiest to decorate.

Here is the step-by-step method for stenciling a cookie (either plain or coated with a smooth icing such as Poured Fondant Icing, page 15):

1. Place the stencil on top of the cookie.
2. Sprinkle decorating sugar over the cookie before baking, or over damp icing on a baked cookie. Or, brush the baked cookie with fondant icing, food coloring, or chocolate.
3. If using sugar, brush any sugar left on the stencil into the cutouts of the stencil.
4. Gently remove the stencil, lifting it straight up.
5. Brush or wipe the stencil clean and decorate the next cookie.

ADDING COLOR

You can add color to your cookies with food colorings, decorating sugars, dusts, and sprinkles, each of which comes in a variety of forms.

Food Colorings

The most common way food colorings are used is for tinting icings. But they can also be used to paint cookies, applied over fully dried Poured Fondant Icing (page 15) or Royal Icing (page 14)

with a clean artist's paintbrush. We recommend paste colors, sold in hobby stores and specialty baking and cake-decorating shops, because they are the most concentrated and you don't need to use much. (Food colorings impart a chemical flavor, so the less used, the better.) Gel colors, available in most supermarkets, are a good choice, as well. Liquid colors will do as long as you don't need a deep, dark color. Some specialty baking and cake-decorating shops carry powdered food colorings, which are similar to paste colors in their color intensity and work wonderfully for dyeing dry ingredients such as sugar.

Food decorating pens that look like ink markers but are filled with food coloring are ideal for inscribing fine lines. Small tubes filled with opaque or gel decorator icing or confectionery coating are also used like pens.

Decorating Sugars

Regular decorating sugar, also called sanding sugar, is a bit coarser than granulated sugar and comes in just about every color imaginable. You'll find the most popular colors in most supermarkets. Crafts stores and hobby shops carry more exotic colors, such as the newer gold and silver metallic sugars that can add a sparkle to angel wings.

As the name implies, coarse decorating sugar (in white and colors) has large grains, which give it a bit more depth and sparkle. We use it on all kinds of cookies, but especially on Sugar Pretzels (page 95) because it resembles the coarse salt used to decorate (noncookie) pretzels.

You can also make your own decorating sugar by working some paste food coloring into granulated sugar with the tines of a fork or your fingertips. (Wear vinyl gloves if you don't want to dye your fingers.) Or, add powdered food coloring to sugar and shake well.

The easiest way to decorate cookies with these sugars is to shake them on, which is why most decorating sugars come in jars with shaker tops. For a little more control, pick up pinches of sugar with your fingertips and sprinkle evenly over the cookie. If you want a solid sugar coating on an iced cookie, make sure the icing is still moist and then lay the cookie, icing side down, in a plate of sugar and shake off the excess.

Edible glitter or sparkling sugar (Wilton's version is called Cake Sparkles) consists of translucent flakes of sugar that sparkle. Against a backdrop of white icing, the flakes resembles freshly fallen snow or shimmering lights, which is why we recommend it for Meringue Snowflakes (page 93) and Twinkling Little Stars (page 239). To apply them, sprinkle them on the cookie or on damp icing, like decorating sugar.

To give cookies a light, even, attractive dusting of confectioners' sugar, place the sugar in a fine-mesh strainer, hold it about twelve inches above the cookies, and shake it gently, tapping the rim of the strainer with your other hand to release an even coating. For a dark dusting on light cookies, do the same with cocoa powder or ground cinnamon.

Dusts

Hobby and crafts stores and specialty baking and cake-decorating shops carry dusts that give hard icings, such as royal or fondant icing, a lustrous shimmer. Sold as Pearl Dust (Wilton), luster dust, petal dust, or platinum dust, they come in different colors. We especially like the gold and silver metallic dusts. Brush them dry onto the icing, or mix them with a little clear vanilla extract or vodka and paint them onto the icing, using an artist's paintbrush in both cases.

Sprinkles

There's an endless supply of sprinkles, tiny confections used to decorate cookies and cakes. They even come in shapes, such as tiny Christmas trees.

- Nonpareils: Tiny, hard sugar balls in various colors.
- Dragées: Larger nonpareils with a shiny coating of silver, gold, copper, or bronze.
- Jimmies: Rod-shaped candies, often chocolate flavored.
- Confetti: Small candy disks that resemble paper confetti.
- Decors: This is a trademark for Cake Mate's mini candy disks.

PRESENTATION AND PACKAGING

The host of the exchange can handle the presentation, arranging the cookies on platters, or displaying them in gift boxes, baskets, or in other imaginative ways. Many of the recipes in this book include ideas for attractively presenting the cookies. It's more fun, though—and saves the host some time—if the cookie exchangers take charge of displaying their own baking efforts. The host can supply blank labels for participants to write the names of their recipe.

At a typical exchange, guests will bring their own containers to take cookies home. Large, self-sealing plastic bags or hard plastic containers make carrying cookies home a snap. If you're hosting the exchange, have some bags or containers on hand for guests who forgot to bring them.

For a more festive, fancy look for transport home, the host or the guests can supply inexpensive gift boxes lined with waxed paper, small Chinese-style takeout containers, cellophane bags (with holiday-themed stickers to seal them), or even cookie tins. (Buy them on sale after the previous year's holidays.)

PARTY THEMES

Christmas doesn't begin and end with cookies. If you're going to throw a holiday party, have some fun. Here are seven ideas for putting together a themed cookie exchange get-together.

BEST CHRISTMAS OUTFIT

Who says the costume fun has to end with Halloween? Award prizes for the goofiest, prettiest, most elegant, or most outrageous holiday outfit.

CHARITABLE DONATIONS

This is a good idea for a larger cookie exchange, such as a holiday party at the office. Ask participants to bring canned goods for the local food pantry or toys for the local toy drive, along with their cookie contribution. Or, have everyone bring one or two dozen cookies for the party, and an additional dozen to be auctioned off, with the proceeds to go to charity. (In most cases, you cannot donate home-baked cookies to local organizations because of health regulations.)

CREATE A COOKIE RECIPE BOX

Ask guests to bring enough copies of their cookie recipe on index cards for every cookie exchanger at the party. Then supply each guest with paints, colored markers, stencils, stickers, and other crafts supplies and a recipe box, so everyone can decorate a box for storing the cards they will be taking home.

CAROLING MARATHON

Who can remember all the stanzas to "Silent Night"—or hold out the longest through endless carols? You might want to run this idea past potential guests before you host the party. Some people understandably run screaming into the night when they hear the five hundredth refrain of "Little Drummer Boy."

CHRISTMAS AROUND THE WORLD

Ask bakers to bring cookies that celebrate an ethnic tradition, preferably reflecting their own ancestry. Or, if everyone is up to a challenge, tell them to bring cookies from an ethnic background they don't know well.

Another idea is to pick one area or country famous for its cookies, such as Scandinavia or Germany, and have everyone bake a different classic from the chosen spot. If the members of your exchange hail from a similar ancestry, they could bring different cookies representing that background. For example, if most of you are of Polish heritage, one person could bring *kolache*, another could bring Polish cheese cookies, another poppy-seed cookies, and so on.

HOLIDAY STORIES

At this get-together, partygoers share stories of their best Christmas. Was it the Christmas that Dad came home from the war? When Santa dropped off a new wardrobe (sewn by Mom) for your favorite doll? When Mom and Dad got you the bike you wanted? When the whole family worked in a food pantry? When you got to sing the solo at midnight Mass?

FOR THE "TROOPS"

Ask participants to bring cookies that stand up well to long-distance mailing and storage. Partygoers can pack "care packages" for soldiers, sailors, students studying overseas, or anyone else who is a long way from home and could use some sweet cheer. Crisp dry cookies, such as biscotti or shortbread, work best.

In addition to these more general party themes, you can build a party around the cookies themselves. In Cookies to Build a Party Around (page 33), you'll find four ideas to do just that.

PARTY MENUS

The menu for a cookie exchange can consist of just cookies and beverages or it can be a more elaborate spread. To save time and speed cleanup, stick to finger foods such as tea sandwiches, boiled shrimp, California rolls, crostini, deviled eggs, fruit-and-cheese skewers, bite-size savory turnovers or mini-quiches, and vegetables with hummus or other dips. Because people will be eating a lot of cookies, it's a good idea to make the rest of the food fairly healthful, stressing vegetables, fruits, and seafood over other richer foods.

For beverages, you can never go wrong with the two classic cookie accompaniments, coffee and milk. You might also like to make a holiday season classic, such as eggnog or mulled wine, or opt for nearly everyone's favorite wintertime beverage, hot chocolate. Following are recipes for six seasonal beverages that will be a hit at any cookie exchange.

EGGNOG

makes **20** (½-cup) servings

If you find traditional eggnog too rich, substitute evaporated low-fat milk for the half-and-half.

8 CUPS HALF-AND-HALF

6 LARGE EGGS, SEPARATED

1⅓ CUPS SUGAR

1 TEASPOON VANILLA EXTRACT

1 TEASPOON GROUND NUTMEG, PLUS EXTRA FOR SPRINKLING

2 CUPS RUM OR BOURBON, OR 2 ADDITIONAL CUPS HALF-AND-HALF PLUS 2 TEASPOONS RUM EXTRACT

1 In a large, heavy, nonaluminum saucepan, whisk together the half-and-half, egg yolks, and sugar until blended. Place over medium heat and cook, stirring occasionally, until the sugar has dissolved and the mixture is steaming hot, 4 to 5 minutes.

2 Remove from the heat and let cool, then stir in the vanilla and the 1 teaspoon nutmeg.

3 In a large bowl, with an electric mixer, beat the egg whites until stiff, glossy peaks form. Fold into the cooled egg yolk mixture.

4 Pour into a pitcher or punch bowl, cover, and chill until very cold. Shortly before serving, stir in the rum and sprinkle nutmeg lightly over the top. Or, put nutmeg in a shaker so guests can sprinkle it to taste on their own serving.

5 Ladle into glasses to serve.

CRANBERRY
WASSAIL

makes
20
(½-cup)
servings

You can use plain cranberry juice cocktail or a blend, such as cranberry-apple or cranberry-raspberry. To keep the wassail warm, set it on a hot plate or keep on the stove over very low heat.

4 WHOLE NUTMEGS

4 SLICES FRESH GINGER

2 CINNAMON STICKS

4 ALLSPICE BERRIES OR WHOLE CLOVES

3 CUPS SWEETENED CRANBERRY JUICE

2 CUPS APPLE JUICE

2 TABLESPOONS HONEY

1 CUP BRANDY OR ADDITIONAL APPLE JUICE

1 Put the nutmegs, ginger, cinnamon, and allspice in the center of a square of cheesecloth and tie the corners together with kitchen twine.

2 In a large, heavy, nonaluminum saucepan, combine the cranberry juice, apple juice, honey, and cheesecloth bundle and bring to a simmer over medium heat. Simmer for 7 to 8 minutes to blend the flavors.

3 Remove from the heat, and remove and discard the spices. Stir in the brandy. Ladle into cups and serve warm.

HOT
MULLED WINE

makes **24** (½-cup) servings

Zinfandel is a good choice for this traditional Christmastime beverage. To keep the mulled wine warm, set it on a hot plate or keep on the stove over very low heat.

24 WHOLE CLOVES, PLUS EXTRA FOR STUDDING ORANGE SLICES

4 CINNAMON STICKS

2 WHOLE NUTMEGS

2 (750-ML) BOTTLES DRY RED WINE

2 CUPS ORANGE JUICE OR LEMONADE

ZEST OF 1 LARGE ORANGE, IN STRIPS

1½ CUPS SUGAR

¾ CUP WATER

2 ORANGES, SLICED

1 Put the cloves, cinnamon sticks, and nutmegs in the center of a square of cheesecloth and tie the corners together with kitchen twine.

2 In a large, heavy, nonaluminum saucepan, combine the wine, orange juice, orange zest, sugar, water, and cheesecloth bundle and bring to a simmer over medium heat, stirring to dissolve the sugar. Simmer for 8 to 10 minutes to blend the flavors.

3 While the wine simmers, stud each orange slice with 3 or 4 cloves.

4 When the wine is ready, remove and discard the cheesecloth bundle. Carefully ladle the hot wine into a deep, heatproof serving bowl. Float the clove-studded orange slices on the wine. Ladle into cups and serve warm.

SPICED TEA
PUNCH

makes
16
(½-cup)
servings

Chai, a blend of tea and spices inspired by the spiced teas of India, is available in many supermarkets these days. Any spiced tea, such as cinnamon or vanilla, will do if chai is unavailable.

4 CUPS WATER

4 CHAI TEA BAGS OR OTHER SPICED TEA

¼ CUP SUGAR

3 CUPS MANGO JUICE OR NECTAR OR ORANGE-MANGO JUICE BLEND

1 CUP ORANGE JUICE

1 ORANGE, PEELED AND THINLY SLICED

1   Bring the water to a boil in a saucepan. Remove from the heat, add the tea bags and sugar, and let stand for 5 minutes. Stir to dissolve the sugar and discard the tea bags.

2   Pour the tea into a large pitcher or punch bowl. Stir in the mango juice and orange juice. Cover and chill well before serving.

3   Just before serving, float the orange slices on the punch. Serve chilled in glasses.

makes
8
(1-cup)
servings

HOT CHOCOLATE

WITH WHIPPED CREAM

If you want to make the whipped cream in advance to save time just before the party begins, you can purchase a commercial stabilizer, which will keep it stiff without separating for several hours. Look for the stabilizer in specialty foods stores and in the baking section of well-stocked supermarkets. Or, you can float a thin mint chocolate candy or a few marshmallows (page 29) on top of the hot chocolate in place of the cream.

WHIPPED CREAM

1 CUP HEAVY CREAM

3 TABLESPOONS SUGAR

1 TEASPOON VANILLA EXTRACT

7 CUPS MILK

1 CUP CHOPPED SEMISWEET CHOCOLATE OR CHOCOLATE CHIPS

3 TABLESPOONS SUGAR

¾ TEASPOON VANILLA EXTRACT

¾ TEASPOON GROUND CINNAMON

¼ TEASPOON GROUND NUTMEG

8 TABLESPOONS DARK RUM (OPTIONAL)

CHOCOLATE SHAVINGS (OPTIONAL)

8 CINNAMON STICKS (OPTIONAL)

1 To make the whipped cream, in a large bowl, with an electric mixer, beat the cream on low speed until it begins to thicken. On high speed, add the sugar and vanilla and beat until stiff peaks form. Cover and refrigerate until serving.

2 In a small, heavy saucepan, scald the milk over medium heat. Whisk in the chocolate until melted and smooth. Remove from the heat.

3 Whisk in the sugar, vanilla, ground cinnamon, and nutmeg until the sugar dissolves. Pour into cups and add 1 tablespoon rum to each cup, if desired. Top each serving with a dollop of whipped cream and chocolate shavings, and slip in a cinnamon stick. Serve right away.

HOT WHITE
CHOCOLATE WITH CINNAMON

makes
12
(1-cup)
servings

Look for a good-quality white chocolate for this recipe (see page 66), one that lists cocoa butter among the ingredients. For an attractive white-on-white presentation, float marshmallows (opposite) on top of each cup.

10 CUPS MILK

1¼ POUNDS WHITE CHOCOLATE, CHOPPED

2 TEASPOONS CLEAR VANILLA EXTRACT

12 CINNAMON STICKS OR CANDY CANES

1 In a heavy saucepan, scald the milk over medium-low heat. Add the chocolate and whisk until melted and smooth.

2 Remove from the heat and stir in the vanilla. Pour into cups, and slip a cinnamon stick into each cup. Serve right away.

HOMEMADE
MARSHMALLOWS

makes 32 marshmallows

Store-bought marshmallows work fine for dark or white hot chocolate, but making your own marshmallows will elevate both beverages and your cookie recipes to a gourmet level. And although they are technically a candy, and not cookies, you could even bring them to a cookie exchange: Cut each marshmallow larger and package together one marshmallow, one graham cracker, and a couple of squares of chocolate for a homemade s'more kit.

⅓ CUP CONFECTIONERS' SUGAR, PLUS MORE SIFTED FOR ROLLING

2 TABLESPOONS POWDERED GELATIN

1¼ CUPS WATER

2 CUPS GRANULATED SUGAR

2 TABLESPOONS LIGHT CORN SYRUP

1 TEASPOON VANILLA EXTRACT, PREFERABLY CLEAR

1 Butter an 8-inch square baking pan. Sprinkle the bottom evenly with the ⅓ cup confectioners' sugar.

2 In a small bowl, sprinkle the gelatin over ½ cup of the water and let stand for 5 minutes to soften, then stir and set aside.

3 In a small, heavy saucepan, combine the granulated sugar, the remaining ¾ cup water, and the corn syrup. Place over low heat and stir until the sugar dissolves. Increase the heat to medium, clip a candy thermometer onto the pan, and cook without stirring until the mixture reaches 260°F (hard-ball stage). Remove from the heat and stir in the gelatin, then the vanilla. Working quickly, pour the mixture into a heatproof bowl and beat with an electric mixer on high speed until fluffy, about 5 minutes.

4 Transfer the mixture to the prepared baking pan, spreading it evenly and smoothing the top with the back of a spoon. Set aside at room temperature until set, 3 to 4 hours.

5 Cut the marshmallow sheet into 32 equal pieces. Put the confectioners' sugar for rolling in a small bowl, and roll each marshmallow in the sugar, coating evenly.

6 Store in an airtight container at room temperature for up to 2 days.

ABOUT THE RECIPES

Here are some tips for making the recipes in this book that will ensure your cookie baking is a success.

Each recipe includes a Cookie Exchange Tip, which gives an idea on how to best prepare, transport, or present the cookie for an exchange.

Unless otherwise noted, all the butter used in recipes is unsalted, all the flour is all-purpose (bleached or unbleached works equally well), and all the eggs are large. For information on the various types of chocolate and cocoa powder used—ingredients that are favorites of Christmastime bakers—see page 66.

We tested the recipes with a stand mixer. If you use a handheld mixer, you may need to adjust the speed upward, plan on some steps taking a little longer, and possibly stir in the dry ingredients by hand.

To prevent cookies from baking up tough, measure the flour precisely (that means dipping the measuring cup into the flour to fill it, then leveling off the top) and do not overmix the dough. Also, when making rolled cookies, do not reroll the scraps too many times. We've found that you can gather up and reroll the scraps twice with no significant difference in the texture of the baked cookies.

We typically use 12-by-17-inch rimmed, heavy-duty aluminum baking sheets. You can use sheet pans with sides or without; we've found that the difference in baking time and evenness is minimal. Cookies will bake faster on darker cookie sheets and slower on double-insulated cookie sheets. The insulated sheets are ideal for meringues and other particularly delicate cookies.

Most recipes call for lightly greasing or spraying the cookie sheets. Use a bit of shortening or butter on a paper towel to grease sheets. Or, spray them evenly with nonstick cooking spray, either plain or butter flavored. If you use nonstick cookie sheets, they usually do not need to be greased. If you are greasing a pan for an unbaked treat, always use butter for the best flavor.

Most ovens will comfortably hold only one cookie sheet at a time. Bake cookies in batches, placing the cookie sheet in the center of the oven, and make sure the cookie sheet is completely cool before putting another batch of cookies on it. If you have a large oven, you can bake two sheets at once. Be sure to rotate them front to back halfway through the cooking time to ensure even baking.

When the cookies are done, remove the cookie sheet from the oven and place it on a wire rack or trivet. Most cookies should remain on the cookie sheet for a minute or two to give them time to firm up. Then, use a thin offset spatula (pancake turner) to remove them to a wire rack to cool completely.

Many of the recipes yield fewer cookies than you may need for an exchange. Most can easily be doubled. Exceptions include madeleines, meringues, and other cookies made with an egg-rich batter.

The yield given for each recipe is approximate. You may end up with slightly more or slightly fewer cookies, depending on how precisely you measure or roll out the dough.

Because you will be making large batches, and you won't always be able to bake the cookies just before the cookie exchange, knowing how to store both cookie dough and baked cookies will come in handy. Here are some general guidelines.

STORING COOKIE DOUGH

One of the joys of making cookies is that you rarely have to bake them all at once. You can leave the dough in the bowl, cover the bowl tightly, and refrigerate it for several hours, or sometimes a day or two. In fact, many doughs require chilling before they can be molded or rolled. Even the dough for some drop cookies, such as chocolate chip, benefits from being chilled, yielding balls with a more uniform shape and rounded profile.

Butter-rich doughs that contain little or no leavening and no eggs, such as many rolled or refrigerator cookies, will keep even longer in the refrigerator if you wrap them airtight. We have held such doughs for 2 or sometimes even 3 weeks.

Doughs that are rich in butter (or other fat) and contain little leavening can be tightly wrapped and frozen for 4 to 6 weeks. Thaw in the refrigerator, then let stand at room temperature until pliable.

Egg-based cookie doughs, such as meringues or madeleines, should be treated like cake batter and baked immediately. Doughs that contain a fairly large amount of leavening, especially baking soda, can be refrigerated briefly, but are best used as soon as possible.

STORING BAKED COOKIES

Two storage rules apply to all cookies: The first is to make sure the cookies are completely cool before you pack them away. If they are not, the steam from the warm cookies will turn the whole batch soggy. The second rule is never to store cookies of different types or flavors together. The moisture from cake-like cookies will cause a batch of crisp cookies to turn soft, and if you store, for example, chocolate and vanilla cookies, or lemon and ginger cookies, in the same container, they may start tasting like each other.

Most cookies keep well in airtight containers for 2 or 3 days at room temperature. Store sticky cookies, such as brownies or cookies iced with buttercream, in a single layer (a cookie sheet with sides is ideal for this), covered with aluminum foil, or layer them, separating the layers with waxed paper.

It might seem fine to pop cookies into a tin and freeze them for 6 months, but 6 to 8 weeks is generally much better. Cookies grow stale and pick up off flavors in the freezer. Rich butter cookies stay fresh longest, and can be frozen for 2 to 3 months if the containers are airtight.

Sticky bar cookies, filled cookies, and soft, cakelike cookies usually do not freeze well. If you are finishing cookies with buttercream, a chocolate glaze, or other sticky topping, freeze them plain and then frost or glaze them just before serving. Or, freeze the frosted or glazed cookies in a single layer on a baking sheet, then layer them, separating the layers with waxed paper, in airtight tins.

PART 2

COOKIES TO BUILD
A PARTY AROUND

CHAPTER 1: DEAR SANTA:
DRESSED-UP CLASSICS 34
Chocolate-Edged Chocolate Chip Cookies 36
Oatmeal Cookies with White Chocolate Chips
    and Dried Cherries 37
Eggnog Snickerdoodles. 39
Animal Sugar Cookies. 40
Xmas M&M's Cookies. 43
Stamped Peanut Butter Cookies 44
Marbled Chocolate–Cream Cheese Brownies 45
Father Christmas S'mores. 46

CHAPTER 2: GINGER AND SPICE 48
Basic Gingerbread. 50
Old Salem Molasses Ginger Cookies 52
Lebkuchen. 54
Double Gingersnaps 56
Ginger Pfeffernuesse. 57
Mini Gingerbread Cupcakes
    with Rum-Raisin Frosting. 58

CHAPTER 3: FOR CHOCOHOLICS 60
Deep, Dark Chocolate Sandwich Cookies. 62
Malted Milk Chocolate Cookies 65
Chocolate-Mint Bars 69
Fudgy Brownie Bites. 71
Mini Devil's Food Cupcakes with
    White Chocolate Filling 72
Cinnamon Chip–Chocolate Chip Cookies 74
Dark Chocolate Cookies Studded with
    White Chocolate 76
Double-Chocolate Chewies. 77

CHAPTER 4: COOKIE ORNAMENTS ... 78
Tuxedoed Gingerbread Polar Bears 80
Candy Cane Cookies 82
Large Cinnamon Dough Angels 84
Hand-Painted Xmas Cookie Rings 89
Mint Meringue Wreaths 91
Meringue Snowflakes 93
Sugar Pretzels. 95
Stained-Glass Ornaments 97
Red-Nosed Rudolph Cookies. 99

CHAPTER
I

DEAR SANTA: DRESSED-UP CLASSICS

For generations, young children have been leaving out a plate of cookies and a glass of milk for Santa (and a carrot or two for Rudolph) on Christmas Eve. After all, running that sleigh all over the world is hard work.

Santa enjoys all kinds of cookies, of course, but you only need to look at him to know that he—and everybody else—likes the classics: chocolate chip, oatmeal, and peanut butter. They speak of home, of after-school snacks with a cold glass of milk, and of late-night raids on the cookie jar. And that's precisely why these same cookies will liven up a cozy gathering of bakers.

But because they are everyday favorites, they don't always seem fancy eough for the holidays. That's easy to take care of—just dress them up.

CHOCOLATE-EDGED

CHOCOLATE CHIP COOKIES

makes about **32** cookies

If when you melt the chocolate chips, the chocolate is too thick for coating the cookie edges thinly and neatly, stir a teaspoon or two of flavorless vegetable oil into the melted chocolate.

COOKIE EXCHANGE TIP: Everyone adores chocolate chip cookies, and rimming the edges with chocolate moves them up to holiday level.

1¼ CUPS ALL-PURPOSE FLOUR

½ TEASPOON BAKING SODA

¼ TEASPOON SALT

½ CUP (1 STICK) UNSALTED BUTTER, AT ROOM TEMPERATURE

½ CUP FIRMLY PACKED BROWN SUGAR

½ CUP GRANULATED SUGAR

1 LARGE EGG

1 TEASPOON VANILLA EXTRACT

1 (12-OUNCE) PACKAGE SEMISWEET CHOCOLATE CHIPS (ABOUT 2 CUPS)

½ CUP CHOPPED WALNUTS OR PECANS, PREFERABLY TOASTED (SEE PAGE 38)

1 Preheat the oven to 375°F. Lightly grease or spray cookie sheets.

2 In a medium bowl, whisk together the flour, baking soda, and salt. Set aside.

3 In a large bowl, with an electric mixer, beat together the butter and brown and granulated sugars on medium speed until light, 2 to 3 minutes. Beat in the egg, then the vanilla. On low speed, gradually beat in the flour mixture just until mixed. Stir in ¾ cup of the chocolate chips and all of the nuts.

4 Drop the dough by rounded teaspoons onto the prepared cookie sheets, spacing them 1½ to 2 inches apart.

5 Bake in the center of the oven until golden, 10 to 12 minutes. Let cool on the cookie sheets for 2 minutes, then transfer to wire racks.

6 When the cookies have cooled, place the remaining chocolate chips (about 1¼ cups) in a microwave-safe bowl or in the top of a double boiler. Microwave at 80 percent power or heat over (not touching) barely simmering water, stirring occasionally, until melted and smooth (see page 67). Let cool slightly.

7 Lightly rotate the edge of each cookie in the melted chocolate. Return to the wire rack and let stand until the chocolate sets.

OATMEAL COOKIES
WITH WHITE CHOCOLATE CHIPS AND DRIED CHERRIES

makes about **48** cookies

You can easily double this recipe for a large cookie exchange.

COOKIE EXCHANGE TIP: Buy an inexpensive gold metallic basket (or paint an old wicker basket with gold spray paint). Line it with a colorful Christmas-print napkin and nestle the cookies in the basket.

2 CUPS ALL-PURPOSE FLOUR

1 TEASPOON BAKING SODA

¾ TEASPOON GROUND CINNAMON

¼ TEASPOON GROUND NUTMEG

¼ TEASPOON SALT

1 CUP (2 STICKS) UNSALTED BUTTER, AT ROOM TEMPERATURE

¼ CUP FIRMLY PACKED LIGHT BROWN SUGAR

2 LARGE EGGS

2 TEASPOONS VANILLA EXTRACT

2½ CUPS QUICK-COOKING (NOT INSTANT) ROLLED OATS

1 CUP WHITE CHOCOLATE CHIPS

½ CUP DRIED TART CHERRIES OR CRANBERRIES

1   Preheat the oven to 325°F. Lightly grease or spray cookie sheets.

2   In a medium bowl, whisk together the flour, baking soda, cinnamon, nutmeg, and salt. Set aside.

3   In a large bowl, with an electric mixer, beat together the butter and sugar on medium speed until light, 2 to 3 minutes. Beat in the eggs, one at time, beating well after each addition, then beat in the vanilla. On low speed, gradually beat in the flour mixture just until mixed. Stir in the oats, chocolate chips, and dried cherries. The dough will be stiff.

4   Drop the dough by rounded teaspoons onto the prepared cookie sheets, spacing them about 2 inches apart.

5   Bake in the center of the oven until firm on top and golden on the bottom, 12 to 15 minutes. Let cool on the cookie sheets for 2 minutes, then transfer to wire racks to cool completely.

TOASTING NUTS AND COCONUT

Toasting nuts and coconut brings out their flavor, and will make cookies that use them taste better. The method for toasting them is similar; only the timing differs. Note that if you are sprinkling nuts on the tops of cookies before baking, you don't need to toast them in advance. They will toast automatically as the cookie bakes.

1. Preheat the oven to 350°F.

2. Spread the nuts (halves or pieces) or the sweetened flaked or shredded coconut in a single layer on a cookie sheet with sides.

3. Toast the nuts, stirring once at the halfway point, until they start to give off a toasted aroma and have taken on some color, 8 to 10 minutes. (The general rule is that if you can smell the nuts, they are ready.) Be careful not to leave them in the oven too long or they will burn.

4. Toast the coconut, stirring once, until it is lightly golden, about 5 minutes.

5. Immediately pour the nuts or coconut into a shallow bowl or plate and let cool.

The skin on hazelnuts (filberts) tends to loosen in the heat of the oven. It is not essential to remove the skins but the nuts will taste better if you do. Wrap the hazelnuts, still warm from the oven, in a clean, dry kitchen towel and rub them vigorously in the towel. Most of the loose skin will flake off the nuts. Don't worry about any stubborn bits that you cannot remove.

EGGNOG
SNICKERDOODLES

makes 48 cookies

Snickerdoodles, sugar cookies with a crackled top popular in the Midwest, are normally dusted with cinnamon sugar. Replacing most of the cinnamon with nutmeg gives the cookies a flavor reminiscent of eggnog.

COOKIE EXCHANGE TIP: Serve these nutmeg-coated sugar cookies with eggnog or with chai lattes.

1¾ CUPS SUGAR

½ TEASPOON GROUND CINNAMON

1½ TEASPOONS GROUND NUTMEG

2⅔ CUPS ALL-PURPOSE FLOUR

1½ TEASPOONS CREAM OF TARTAR

1 TEASPOON BAKING SODA

¼ TEASPOON SALT

½ CUP (1 STICK) UNSALTED BUTTER, AT ROOM TEMPERATURE

½ CUP VEGETABLE SHORTENING

2 LARGE EGGS

2 TEASPOONS RUM EXTRACT

1 Preheat the oven to 375°F. Lightly grease or spray cookie sheets.

2 In a small bowl, stir together ¼ cup of the sugar, the cinnamon, and the nutmeg. Set aside.

3 In a medium bowl, whisk together the flour, cream of tartar, baking soda, and salt. Set aside.

4 In a large bowl, with an electric mixer, beat together the butter, shortening, and the remaining 1½ cups sugar on medium speed until light, 2 to 3 minutes. Beat in the eggs, one at a time, beating well after each addition, then beat in the rum extract. On low speed, gradually beat in the flour mixture just until mixed.

5 Pinch off pieces of the dough and roll between your palms into 1¼-inch balls. (If the dough is too soft to handle, refrigerate it for 15 to 30 minutes and try again.) Roll the balls in the cinnamon-nutmeg sugar to coat evenly. Place on the prepared cookie sheets, spacing them at least 1½ inches apart.

6 Bake in the center of the oven until golden and cracked on top, 10 to 12 minutes. Let cool on the cookie sheets for 2 minutes, then transfer to wire racks to cool completely.

ANIMAL

SUGAR COOKIES

makes about
24
cookies

Use your imagination—and as many "tools" as you like—to make a batch of highly decorated cookies.

COOKIE EXCHANGE TIP: Use at least a 4-inch cookie cutter. Each cookie becomes a work of art. At the exchange, try to negotiate for 2 smaller cookies for each of your jeweled "animals."

2½ CUPS ALL-PURPOSE FLOUR

1 TEASPOON BAKING POWDER

½ TEASPOON SALT

¾ CUP (1½ STICKS) UNSALTED BUTTER, AT ROOM TEMPERATURE

1 CUP SUGAR

2 LARGE EGGS

1 TEASPOON LEMON OR VANILLA EXTRACT

EASY VANILLA ICING (PAGE 16)

FOOD COLORING IN COLOR(S) OF CHOICE (OPTIONAL)

SLICED ALMONDS; RED CANDIED CHERRIES, CUT IN HALF; SPRINKLES; NONPAREILS; AND/OR DECORATING PENS FOR DECORATING

1   In a medium bowl, whisk together the flour, baking powder, and salt. Set aside.

2   In a large bowl, with an electric mixer, beat together the butter and sugar on medium speed until light, 2 to 3 minutes. Beat in the eggs, one at a time, beating well after each addition, and then beat in the lemon extract. On low speed, beat in the flour mixture until a smooth dough forms.

3   Gather the dough into a ball, pat into a thick disk, and wrap in plastic wrap. Refrigerate until firm, about 2 hours.

4   Preheat the oven to 350°F. Have ready ungreased cookie sheets.

5   Place the dough on a lightly floured pastry cloth or board, and roll out ¼ inch thick. Using a 4-inch animal-shaped cookie cutter, cut out cookies. Giraffe, camel, and/or elephant cutters are fun. Using a spatula, transfer the cookies to the cookie sheets, spacing them about 1½ inches apart. Gather the scraps, reroll, and cut out more cookies.

continued...

. . . *continued*

6 Bake in the center of the oven until faintly golden, 8 to 10 minutes. Let cool on the cookie sheets for about 3 minutes, then transfer to wire racks to cool completely.

7 Make the icing as directed. If you want to make your "animals" different colors, divide the icing into batches and tint each batch with food coloring as desired.

8 Using an icing spatula, ice the cookies. While the icing is still moist, decorate the cookies as desired. After the icing has set, use decorating pens to add details or to outline the cookies.

M&M'S COOKIES

makes about
20
cookies

For more evenly shaped cookies, refrigerate the dough until it is easy to handle, then roll between your palms into balls.

COOKIE EXCHANGE TIP: These big, colorful cookies, made with green and red candies, look great served in a large cookie tin. Choose a tin attractively decorated in holiday colors, arrange the cookies in the open tin, and prop up the lid against the rim so its design shows.

¾ CUP ALL-PURPOSE FLOUR

¼ TEASPOON BAKING POWDER

¼ TEASPOON SALT

½ CUP VEGETABLE SHORTENING

½ CUP FIRMLY PACKED LIGHT BROWN SUGAR

1 LARGE EGG

½ TEASPOON VANILLA EXTRACT

¾ CUP MIXED RED AND GREEN M&M'S

¾ CUP OLD-FASHIONED OR QUICK COOKING (NOT INSTANT) ROLLED OATS

1 Preheat the oven to 350°F. Lightly grease or spray cookie sheets.

2 In a medium bowl, whisk together the flour, baking powder, and salt. Set aside.

3 In a large bowl, with an electric mixer, beat together the shortening and sugar on medium speed until light, 2 to 3 minutes. Beat in the egg, then the vanilla. On low speed, gradually beat in the flour mixture just until mixed. Gently stir in the M&M's and oats. The dough will be stiff.

4 Drop the dough by heaping tablespoons onto the prepared cookie sheets, spacing them about 2 inches apart. Press each cookie lightly with the bottom of a drinking glass.

5 Bake in the center of the oven until firm on top and lightly golden on the bottom, 10 to 12 minutes. Let cool on the cookie sheets for about 2 minutes, then transfer to wire racks to cool completely.

STAMPED
PEANUT BUTTER COOKIES

makes
48
cookies

Traditionally, peanut butter cookies are decorated by creating a simple crisscross pattern with fork tines in the top of each cookie. At Christmastime, a cookie stamp with a holiday-themed design creates a more festive presentation.

COOKIE EXCHANGE TIP: For the best results, use a cookie stamp with a simple design, such as a snowflake or holly sprig.

1½ CUPS ALL-PURPOSE FLOUR

½ TEASPOON BAKING SODA

¼ TEASPOON SALT

½ CUP (1 STICK) UNSALTED BUTTER, AT ROOM TEMPERATURE

½ CUP CREAMY PEANUT BUTTER

⅔ CUP GRANULATED SUGAR

⅓ CUP FIRMLY PACKED LIGHT BROWN SUGAR

1 LARGE EGG

½ TEASPOON VANILLA EXTRACT

1   Preheat the oven to 375°F. Lightly grease or spray cookie sheets.

2   In a medium bowl, whisk together the flour, baking soda, and salt. Set aside.

3   In a large bowl, with an electric mixer, beat together the butter, peanut butter, and granulated and brown sugars on medium speed until light, about 2 minutes. Beat in the egg, then the vanilla. On low speed, gradually beat in the flour mixture just until mixed. The dough will be stiff.

4   Pinch off pieces of the dough and roll between your palms into 1-inch balls. Place on the cookie sheets, spacing them about 1⅛ inches apart. Oil a cookie stamp and press down lightly on a ball to imprint the design. Repeat, oiling the stamp again after stamping every few cookies.

5   Bake in the center of the oven until the edges begin to turn golden, 8 to 10 minutes. Let cool on the cookie sheets for about 1 minute, then transfer to wire racks to cool completely.

MARBLED CHOCOLATE–CREAM CHEESE
BROWNIES

Forgot to buy the cream cheese? Make just the chocolate layer for plain brownies.

COOKIE EXCHANGE TIP: These marbled gems look great arranged on a plain, shiny red plate. When packing them for transport, separate the layers with sheets of waxed paper to keep them from sticking together.

CHOCOLATE BATTER

1 CUP (2 STICKS) UNSALTED BUTTER, CUT INTO CHUNKS

4 OUNCES UNSWEETENED BAKING CHOCOLATE, CHOPPED

1⅔ CUPS SUGAR

3 LARGE EGGS, LIGHTLY BEATEN

1 TEASPOON VANILLA EXTRACT

¼ TEASPOON SALT

1 CUP ALL-PURPOSE FLOUR

CREAM CHEESE BATTER

1 (8-OUNCE) PACKAGE CREAM CHEESE, SOFTENED

½ CUP SUGAR

1 LARGE EGG

½ TEASPOON VANILLA EXTRACT

¼ CUP ALL-PURPOSE FLOUR

1 Preheat the oven to 350°F. Lightly grease or spray a 9-by-13-inch baking pan.

2 Prepare the chocolate batter. Place the butter and chocolate in a microwave-safe bowl or in the top of a double boiler. Microwave at 80 percent power or heat over (not touching) barely simmering water, stirring occasionally, until melted and smooth (see page 67). Let cool slightly.

3 Stir in the sugar until fully combined, then the eggs, vanilla, and salt. Stir in the flour just until mixed. Spread the batter evenly over the bottom of the prepared pan.

4 Prepare the cream cheese batter. In a bowl, with a wooden spoon, beat together the cream cheese, sugar, egg, vanilla, and flour until smooth.

5 Drop the cream cheese batter by spoonfuls evenly over the chocolate layer. Run the tip of a butter knife lightly through the batters to make a dark-and-light marbled design.

6 Bake in the center of the oven until a tester inserted in the center comes out with just a few moist crumbs clinging to it, 30 to 35 minutes. Let cool completely in the pan on a wire rack, then cut into bars and remove from the pan with a small offset spatula or an icing spatula.

FATHER CHRISTMAS
S'MORES

First, we baked star-shaped graham crackers, making each one just large enough to hold a large commercial marshmallow, coated the marshmallows with chocolate, and our s'mores were delicious. Then, we thought of how to make them better. This time we used a slim 3-inch Santa-shaped cookie cutter, made our own marshmallows, and drizzled our silky smooth chocolate over the top. The s'mores were outstanding.

If you don't have a Santa-shaped cutter, you can use a 2-inch star or round cutter, and put the marshmallow in the center. If you are pressed for time, use store-bought marshmallows and graham crackers, and the s'mores will still be a hit.

COOKIE EXCHANGE TIP: Handle these irresistible s'mores carefully. Arrange them in a single layer in the bottom of a large, flat box or several flat boxes, depending on how many you make.

1 (12-OUNCE) PACKAGE MILK CHOCOLATE OR SEMISWEET CHOCOLATE CHIPS (ABOUT 2 CUPS)

1 TABLESPOON LIGHT CORN SYRUP

30 TO 32 HOMEMADE MARSHMALLOWS (PAGE 29)

30 TO 32 SANTA GRAHAMS (PAGE 151)

1 Place the chocolate in a microwave-safe bowl or in the top of a double boiler. Microwave at 80 percent power or heat over (not touching) barely simmering water, stirring occasionally, until melted and smooth (see page 67). Stir in the corn syrup.

2 Using a pastry brush, dab the bottom of a marshmallow with a little of the melted chocolate, and set the marshmallow on a graham cracker, putting it over the bag of toys. Repeat until all the graham crackers are topped with a marshmallow. Place the graham crackers on wire racks set over a sheet of waxed paper or parchment paper to catch any drips.

3 Drizzle about 2 teaspoons of the cooled chocolate over each marshmallow. Let stand until set.

CHAPTER
2

GINGER AND SPICE

A specialty of the holiday season, ginger-bread, heady with sweet, warm spices, has been baked in northern and central Europe for centuries. Its texture can vary from crisp to cakelike, and its shape might be a simple round or square, sometimes impressed with a design, or more elaborate figures of men, women, or animals, oftentimes fancifully decorated. Gingerbread is wonderfully versatile, too: sturdy enough for building a house and tender enough to be a great eating cookie. Its equally fragrant cousins, gingersnaps, *Lebkuchen*, and *Pfeffernuesse*, are also indispensable treats of the holiday season.

For a fun cookie exchange activity, have your guests build and decorate a gingerbread house, using either plans you have made yourself or a purchased house kit.

BASIC

GINGERBREAD

makes about
16
cookies

This is a good all-purpose, dark, spicy gingerbread. It's tasty, keeps well, and is sturdy enough to use for everything from gingerbread people to gingerbread houses. For cookies that will be eaten, use butter for the best flavor. For ginger-bread houses or other decorative cookies that probably won't be eaten, vegetable shortening can be used.

COOKIE EXCHANGE TIP: Turn this batch of gingerbread dough into Red-Nosed Rudolph Cookies (page 99) or Tuxedoed Gingerbread Polar Bears (page 80). Or, stick with tradition and cut out gingerbread men and women and decorate with icing.

5 CUPS ALL-PURPOSE FLOUR, PLUS MORE AS NEEDED

1 TEASPOON BAKING SODA

½ TEASPOON SALT

1 TABLESPOON GROUND GINGER

2 TEASPOONS GROUND CINNAMON

½ TEASPOON GROUND ALLSPICE OR NUTMEG

1 CUP (2 STICKS) UNSALTED BUTTER OR VEGETABLE SHORTENING, AT ROOM TEMPERATURE

1 CUP SUGAR

¾ CUP UNSULFURED MOLASSES

1 LARGE EGG

1 TEASPOON VANILLA EXTRACT

ROYAL ICING (PAGE 14) OR STORE-BOUGHT DECORATOR ICING

SPRINKLES AND MINI CANDIES FOR DECORATING

1   In a medium bowl, whisk together the flour, baking soda, salt, ginger, cinnamon, and allspice. Set aside.

2   In a large bowl, with an electric mixer, beat together the butter and sugar on medium speed until light, 2 to 3 minutes. Beat in the molasses, egg, and vanilla. On low speed, gradually beat in the flour mixture just until mixed. The dough will be medium-stiff but sticky. If it is too soft, beat in additional flour, a tablespoon at a time.

3   Divide the dough in half. Pat each half into a thick disk and wrap separately in plastic wrap. Refrigerate until firm, at least 1 hour or up to 1 day. Let stand at room temperature for 10 minutes before rolling.

4   Preheat the oven to 350°F. Lightly grease or spray cookie sheets.

5   Place 1 dough disk on a lightly floured pastry cloth or board, and roll
    out ¼ inch thick. Using 4-inch people-shaped cookie cutters or other
    shapes of choice, cut out cookies. Using a large spatula, carefully
    transfer the cookies to a prepared cookie sheet, spacing them about
    1½ inches apart. Repeat with the second dough disk. Combine the
    scraps, reroll, and cut out more cookies.

6   Bake in the center of the oven until firm and just turning golden on
    the edges, 10 to 15 minutes. Let cool on the cookie sheets for 1 to
    2 minutes, then transfer to wire racks to cool completely.

7   Decorate the cooled cookies with the icing and the sprinkles and
    candies as desired.

OLD SALEM
MOLASSES GINGER COOKIES

makes
20
cookies

This recipe traces its ancestry to Old Salem, a Moravian settlement near Winston-Salem, North Carolina, that dates to the mid-seventeenth century. The cookies are a little softer and chewier than Basic Gingerbread (page 50).

COOKIE EXCHANGE TIP: These Old Salem cookies are large, so they may be worth two cookies if you are exchanging them for smaller ones.

3 CUPS ALL-PURPOSE FLOUR, PLUS MORE AS NEEDED

1 TEASPOON BAKING SODA

4 TEASPOONS PUMPKIN PIE SPICE

1 TEASPOON GROUND GINGER

1 CUP UNSULFURED MOLASSES, PREFERABLY DARK (ROBUST)

¼ CUP VEGETABLE SHORTENING

¼ CUP FIRMLY PACKED DARK BROWN SUGAR

2 TABLESPOONS DARK RUM OR ORANGE JUICE

DECORATING SUGAR FOR SPRINKLING

1   In a medium bowl, whisk together the flour, baking soda, pumpkin pie spice, and ginger. Set aside.

2   In a large bowl, with an electric mixer, beat together the molasses, shortening, brown sugar, and rum on medium speed until light, 2 to 3 minutes. On low speed, add half of the flour mixture and beat just until mixed. Then add the remaining flour mixture and beat just until mixed. The dough should be medium-stiff. If it is too soft and sticky, add more flour, a tablespoon at a time.

3   Divide the dough in half. Pat each half into a thick disk and wrap separately in plastic wrap. Refrigerate until firm, at least 2 hours or up to 1 day.

4   Preheat the oven to 350°F. Lightly grease or spray cookie sheets.

5   Place 1 disk dough on a floured pastry cloth or board, and roll out ¼ inch thick. Using a 3-inch round cookie cutter, cut out cookies. Using a large spatula, carefully transfer the cookies to a prepared cookie sheet, spacing them about 2 inches apart. Sprinkle with the decorating sugar. Repeat with the second dough disk. Combine the scraps, reroll, and cut out more cookies.

6   Bake in the center of the oven until just firm to the touch, about 10 minutes. The cookies should not brown. Let cool on the cookie sheets for 2 minutes, then transfer to wire racks to cool completely.

LEBKUCHEN

makes
40
cookies

There are as many varieties of this popular cookie as there are long German words: some crisp, some chewy, some soft and cakelike. Our cookies are chewy. Store them with apple or orange slices for a day or so to keep them from getting too hard. The fruit also improves their flavor.

COOKIE EXCHANGE TIP: We like to arrange these cookie stars on a plate with woven-straw star ornaments interspersed among them.

1 CUP HONEY, PREFERABLY CLOVER OR ORANGE BLOSSOM

3 TABLESPOONS UNSALTED BUTTER, CUT INTO CHUNKS

¾ CUP FIRMLY PACKED LIGHT BROWN SUGAR

1 LARGE EGG

3 CUPS ALL-PURPOSE FLOUR

½ TEASPOON BAKING SODA

1 TEASPOON GROUND CINNAMON

1 TEASPOON GROUND NUTMEG

¼ TEASPOON GROUND CLOVES

¼ CUP MINCED CANDIED LEMON OR ORANGE PEEL, OR A MIXTURE, PLUS MORE FOR GARNISH (OPTIONAL)

½ CUP FINELY CHOPPED ALMONDS OR HAZELNUTS, PREFERABLY TOASTED (SEE PAGE 38)

2 APPLE OR ORANGE SLICES

POURED FONDANT ICING (PAGE 15)

1   In a medium saucepan, bring the honey to a simmer. Stir in the butter until melted, then stir in the brown sugar until smooth. Remove from the heat. Beat in the egg. Set aside.

2   In a large bowl, whisk together the flour, baking soda, cinnamon, nutmeg, and cloves. Add the honey mixture and stir just until mixed. Stir in the ¼ cup candied peel and the nuts. The dough will be sticky.

3   Gather the dough into a ball, pat into a thick disk, and wrap in plastic wrap. Refrigerate overnight.

4   Preheat the oven to 350°F. Lightly grease or spray cookie sheets.

5   Place the dough on a floured pastry cloth or board, and roll out about ⅓ inch thick. The dough will be a bit sticky, and you may need to use a little more flour than usual. Using a 2-inch star-shaped cookie cutter, cut out cookies. Using a spatula, transfer the cookies to the prepared cookie sheets, spacing them about 1½ inches apart. Gather the scraps, reroll, and cut out more cookies.

6 Bake in the center of the oven until no imprint remains when you press the cookies lightly with a fingertip, 10 to 12 minutes. Let cool on the cookie sheets for 2 minutes, then transfer to wire racks to cool completely.

7 Store in an airtight container for a day or two with the apple slices, then remove the cookies from the container and discard the apple slices. (This helps flavor the cookies and gives them their chewy-soft texture.)

8 Brush the cookies with the fondant icing, and sprinkle a little candied peel on each cookie while the icing is still moist. Let the cookies stand until the icing sets. Return the cookies to the airtight container, without the apple slices, for keeping.

DOUBLE
GINGERSNAPS

makes about 45 cookies

These are gingery and crunchy—just like good gingersnaps should be. They keep well, too, making them great for baking in advance and freezing or for mailing.

COOKIE EXCHANGE TIP: Serve these on a holiday-themed plate, with chopped crystallized ginger scattered around the rim.

2½ CUPS ALL-PURPOSE FLOUR

1 TABLESPOON GROUND GINGER

1 TEASPOON GROUND CINNAMON

1 TEASPOON BAKING SODA

¼ TEASPOON SALT

1 CUP (2 STICKS) UNSALTED BUTTER, AT ROOM TEMPERATURE

1 CUP SUGAR

⅔ CUP UNSULFURED MOLASSES

¼ CUP FINELY MINCED CRYSTALLIZED GINGER

1   Preheat the oven to 375°F. Lightly grease or spray cookie sheets.

2   In a medium bowl, whisk together the flour, ground ginger, cinnamon, baking soda, and salt. Set aside.

3   In a large bowl, with an electric mixer, beat together the butter and sugar on medium speed until light, 2 to 3 minutes. Beat in the molasses. On low speed, gradually beat in the flour mixture just until mixed. The dough will be medium-firm and not too sticky.

4   Pinch off pieces of the dough and roll between your palms into balls slightly smaller than 1 inch in diameter. Place on the prepared cookie sheets, spacing them about 1⅛ inches apart. Press each ball lightly with the bottom of a drinking glass, then top each cookie with a few pieces of crystallized ginger.

5   Bake in the center of the oven until slightly flattened, crackled on top, and golden on the bottom, 9 to 11 minutes. Let cool on the cookie sheets for 2 minutes, then transfer to wire racks to cool completely.

GINGER
PFEFFERNUESSE

makes
45
cookies

Pfeffernuesse, or "pepper nuts," are exactly what their name implies, small nutlike cookies lightly flavored with pepper. If the dough sticks to your hands when you're rolling it into balls, dust your hands with flour.

COOKIE EXCHANGE TIP: Mound these cookies in the center of a holiday-decorated plate, then dust with additional confectioners' sugar to suggest snow.

1 CUP GRANULATED SUGAR

3 LARGE EGGS

3 CUPS ALL-PURPOSE FLOUR

¼ TEASPOON WHITE PEPPER

1 TEASPOON GROUND CINNAMON OR CARDAMOM

¼ CUP GROUND ALMONDS

½ CUP CHOPPED CRYSTALLIZED GINGER

SIFTED CONFECTIONERS' SUGAR FOR ROLLING

1 Preheat the oven to 350°F. Lightly grease or spray cookie sheets.

2 In a large bowl, with an electric mixer, beat together the granulated sugar and eggs on high speed until light, 2 to 3 minutes. On low speed, gradually beat in the flour just until mixed. Beat in the pepper, cinnamon, almonds, and ginger until incorporated. The dough will be medium-stiff.

3 Pinch off pieces of the dough and roll between your palms into 1-inch balls. Place on the prepared cookie sheets, spacing them about 1½ inches apart.

4 Bake in the center of the oven until firm to the touch but still pale, 12 to 15 minutes. Let cool for 2 minutes on the cookie sheets, then roll them in the confectioners' sugar to coat evenly. Transfer to wire racks to cool completely.

MINI GINGERBREAD
CUPCAKES WITH RUM-RAISIN FROSTING

makes
24
mini cupcakes

This is a firm cake-style gingerbread that packs a nice kick.

COOKIE EXCHANGE TIP: Bring these mini cupcakes to an exchange for a fun alternative to cookies. Use Christmas-themed cupcake liners.

2½ CUPS ALL-PURPOSE FLOUR

2 TEASPOONS BAKING SODA

¼ TEASPOON SALT

2 TEASPOONS GROUND GINGER

½ CUP (1 STICK) UNSALTED BUTTER

¼ CUP FIRMLY PACKED DARK BROWN SUGAR

2 LARGE EGGS

1 CUP UNSULFURED DARK (ROBUST) MOLASSES

1 CUP BOILING WATER

RUM-RAISIN FROSTING

½ CUP DARK RAISINS

¼ CUP DARK RUM

1 (8-OUNCE) PACKAGE CREAM CHEESE, AT ROOM TEMPERATURE, CUT INTO SMALL PIECES

4 TABLESPOONS (½ STICK) UNSALTED BUTTER, AT ROOM TEMPERATURE, CUT INTO 4 PIECES

2 CUPS SIFTED CONFECTIONERS' SUGAR

1 Preheat the oven to 375°F. Line 24 mini muffin cups with cupcake liners.

2 In a medium bowl, sift together the flour, baking soda, salt, and ginger. Set aside.

3 In a large bowl, with an electric mixer, beat together the butter and brown sugar until creamy, about 2 minutes. Beat in the eggs and then the molasses until well combined. Immediately stir in the boiling water. On low speed, add the flour mixture and mix until smooth.

4 Spoon the batter into the prepared muffin cups, filling them about two-thirds full. Bake in the center of the oven until a toothpick inserted into the center of a cupcake comes out clean and dry, about 20 minutes. Let cool completely in the pan(s) on a wire rack.

5 While the cupcakes are baking and cooling, prepare the frosting. In a small bowl, mix together the raisins and rum and let stand for 15 minutes. Strain, reserving liquid.

6 In a food processor, combine the cream cheese and butter and process until smooth. Add the confectioners' sugar and pulse until a smooth, spreadable frosting forms. Transfer to a bowl. Stir the raisin liquid into the frosting until evenly combined.

7 When the cupcakes are cool, tip them out of the pan(s) and frost them with the frosting. Top with raisins.

CHAPTER
3

FOR CHOCOHOLICS

There's chocolate. And then there's *chocolate*. Many of the recipes in this book contain chocolate, but the recipes in this chapter offer that extra dose to satisfy the diehard chocoholic. Some people are allergic to chocolate and some don't like it, so turn to these pages when you know you will be baking for a small group of chocolate enthusiasts.

Here, you'll find a devil's food cake shrunk to cupcake size and filled with a luscious white chocolate cream, a brownie disguised as a drop cookie, and dark chocolate cookies laced with white chocolate chips, among other irresistible treats to tempt the true chocoholic.

Chocolates, like wine, can range from awful to sublime. To ensure your cookies are as good as they can be, always purchase the best chocolate you can afford.

DEEP, DARK CHOCOLATE
SANDWICH COOKIES

Use unsweetened dark cocoa powder (see page 66) in these wafers. Its deep color makes them almost black.

COOKIE EXCHANGE TIP: For a stunning contrast, decorate the tops of these cookies with Royal Icing (page 14). Pressed for time or need more cookies for a larger exchange? Skip the filling and dust the wafers with sifted confectioners' sugar or drizzle them with melted bittersweet chocolate or Royal Icing.

CHOCOLATE WAFERS

1½ CUPS ALL-PURPOSE FLOUR

⅔ CUP UNSWEETENED DARK COCOA POWDER

¾ TEASPOON BAKING POWDER

¼ TEASPOON SALT

1 CUP SUGAR

2 TABLESPOONS SWEETENED FLAKED OR SHREDDED COCONUT

¾ CUP (1½ STICKS) UNSALTED BUTTER, AT ROOM TEMPERATURE

2 LARGE EGG YOLKS

½ TEASPOON VANILLA EXTRACT

CHOCOLATE BUTTERCREAM (PAGE 17) MADE WITH UNSWEETENED DARK COCOA POWDER

1 Prepare the wafers. In a medium bowl, whisk together the flour, cocoa powder, baking powder, and salt. Set aside.

2 In a food processor or blender, combine the sugar and coconut and process on high speed until the coconut is very finely minced and blended with the sugar. (Or, finely mince the coconut by hand with some of the sugar, then combine with the remaining sugar.)

3 In a large bowl, with an electric mixer, beat together the butter and the sugar-coconut mixture on medium speed until light, 2 to 3 minutes. Beat in the egg yolks and then the vanilla. On low speed, gradually beat in the flour mixture just until mixed. The dough will be stiff.

4 Gather the dough into a ball, pat into a thick disk, and wrap in plastic wrap. Refrigerate until firm, at least 2 hours or up to 2 days.

5 Preheat the oven to 350°F. Lightly grease or spray cookie sheets.

continued...

. . . *continued*

6   Place the dough on a lightly floured pastry cloth or board, and roll out ⅛ inch thick. Using a 2-inch round cookie cutter, cut out cookies. Using a spatula, transfer the cookies to the prepared cookie sheets, spacing them about 1 inch apart. Gather the scraps, reroll, and cut out more cookies.

7   Bake in the center of the oven until no imprint remains when you press the cookies lightly with a fingertip, 8 to 10 minutes. Let cool on the cookie sheets for 2 minutes, then transfer to wire racks to cool completely.

8   When the cookies are cool, turn half of the cookies flat side up. Spread 2 teaspoons buttercream on each upturned cookie. Top with the remaining cookies, flat side down, pressing gently to adhere.

MALTED MILK
CHOCOLATE COOKIES

makes
48
cookies

These chocolaty cookies taste like richer versions of malted milk balls, for the kid in all of us.

COOKIE EXCHANGE TIP: These rich cookies can be sticky, so arrange them in a single layer. A rectangular tray makes this easier. Cover with aluminum foil and keep cool.

1 CUP (2 STICKS) UNSALTED BUTTER, AT ROOM TEMPERATURE

½ CUP SUGAR

1 LARGE EGG

1½ TEASPOONS VANILLA EXTRACT

¾ CUP PLAIN MALTED MILK POWDER

½ TEASPOON SALT

2 CUPS ALL-PURPOSE FLOUR

8 OUNCES MILK CHOCOLATE, CHOPPED

1 TEASPOON FLAVORLESS VEGETABLE OIL

1 Preheat the oven to 350°F. Have ready ungreased cookie sheets.

2 In a large bowl, using an electric mixer, beat together the butter and sugar on medium speed until light, 2 to 3 minutes. Beat in the egg and vanilla, and then beat in the malted milk powder and salt. On low speed, gradually beat in the flour just until mixed. The dough will be stiff.

3 Pinch off pieces of the dough and roll between your palms into 1-inch balls. Place on the cookie sheets, spacing them about 1½ inches apart.

4 Bake in the center of the oven until set on top when lightly tested with a fingertip and golden on the bottom, 12 to 15 minutes. Let cool on the cookie sheets for 2 minutes, then transfer to wire racks to cool completely.

5 When the cookies are cool, place the chocolate in a microwave-safe bowl or in the top of a double boiler. Microwave at 50 percent power or heat over (not touching) barely simmering water, stirring occasionally, until melted and smooth (see page 67). Stir in the oil to create a good coating consistency.

6 Dip the top of each cookie in the melted chocolate, swirling to coat the top completely, and return to the racks. Or, use the back of a teaspoon to spread the melted chocolate over the top of each cookie. Let the cookies stand until the chocolate sets. If the kitchen is warm, you can refrigerate the cookies for about 10 minutes to set the chocolate.

COCOA POWDER AND CHOCOLATE

Unsweetened cocoa powder comes in three types: natural, or nonalkalized; alkalized (also called Dutch process or dutched); and dark cocoa powder, which is a blend of the two. We use the dark cocoa blend, readily available in supermarkets, for recipes where we want a deep, dark chocolate color and rich flavor. If a recipe does not specify which type of cocoa powder to use, natural cocoa powder is preferred, though Dutch-process cocoa is acceptable.

Dark chocolates vary according to the amount of cacao liquor (also called chocolate liquor) they contain, referred to as cacao (or cocoa) content. In the United States, chocolate labeled semisweet or bittersweet must contain a minimum of 35 percent cacao. Most bittersweet chocolate contains at least 50 percent cacao and the best ones have a much higher percentage. When we call for bittersweet chocolate—which is ideal for dipping and coating—we mean chocolate with a 60 to 70 percent cacao content. Most semisweet chocolates have a somewhat lower cacao content, usually 40 to 50 percent. Unsweetened baking chocolate (also known as unsweetened chocolate or baking chocolate) is pure chocolate liquor and, as its name implies, contains no sugar.

German sweet chocolate (sometimes labeled sweet chocolate or dark chocolate), which is a blend of chocolate liquor, cocoa butter, sugar, and flavorings, must have a cacao content of at least 15 percent. Milk chocolate, a blend of chocolate liquor, milk solids, sugar, cocoa butter, and flavorings, contains at least 10 percent cacao.

White chocolate is a mixture of cocoa butter, milk solids, sugar, and flavorings. It must contain at least 20 percent cocoa butter. White coating, often labeled simply "premium white" with no mention of chocolate, is made with palm kernel oil rather than cocoa butter, and can be melted and used for dipping in place of white chocolate. For a white chocolate ganache or filling, however, be sure to use real white chocolate, not white coating. Most of the white baking chips sold in supermarkets do not contain cocoa butter.

Chocolate scorches easily, so you need to keep an eye on it when you are melting it. Also, a drop or two of moisture can cause the chocolate to "seize," or stiffen and become grainy. Make sure the vessel you use for melting is completely dry, and if you are using a double boiler, make sure the steam created by the heating of the water does not reach the chocolate.

MELTING CHOCOLATE

To melt chocolate, chop it or break it into small pieces and place in a microwave-safe bowl or glass measuring cup. To melt dark chocolate (unsweetened, semi-sweet, or bittersweet), microwave at 80 percent power (medium-high) until the chocolate looks softened and shiny but still lumpy. This can take anywhere from 45 seconds to 2 minutes, depending on the amount of chocolate and your oven wattage. The chocolate should become smooth and liquid when you stir it for a while. If the chocolate does not liquefy when stirred for 1 minute, return it to the microwave and check it every 10 seconds, stirring each time, until it is smooth.

To melt white chocolate, milk chocolate, or German sweet chocolate, which burn more easily than dark chocolate because of their higher sugar content, microwave at 50 percent (medium) power until softened and shiny. Stir the chocolate for a minute. If it does not melt completely, continue to microwave, checking it every 10 seconds and stirring each time, until smooth.

You can also melt any type of chocolate in a double boiler. Place the chocolate pieces in the top of a double boiler over (not touching) simmering water and heat, stirring occasionally, until the chocolate is mostly melted but still lumpy. Stir until smooth.

You can use chocolate chips for melting, but keep in mind that they are designed to hold their shape and yield a thicker liquid when melted. If the melted chocolate is a bit too thick for coating, stir in a little flavorless vegetable oil (about 1 teaspoon per cup of chips).

CHOCOLATE-MINT BARS

Virginia varies the cookies she makes every Christmas, but her friends and family would riot if she didn't include these luscious, candylike cookies. They require no baking, but they require chilling and assembly that do take time.

For the crust, we use Nabisco Famous wafers, which are available at many supermarkets. If you don't find them in the cookie aisle, check the ice cream aisle. These dark chocolate wafers are often sold as ice cream mix-ins. If you can't find them, make your own chocolate wafers (page 62).

COOKIE EXCHANGE TIP: Although it's extra work, piping a small design in buttercream atop these cookies makes them look like they came from a fancy bakery. We tint vanilla buttercream pale green and use a small leaf tip. To extend the theme, garnish the plate with tiny fresh mint sprigs.

CRUST

1 (9-OUNCE) PACKAGE DARK CHOCOLATE WAFER COOKIES, FINELY CRUSHED (2 CUPS CRUMBS), OR 2 CUPS GRAHAM CRACKER CRUMBS MIXED WITH 1 TABLESPOON UNSWEETENED COCOA POWDER

½ CUP (1 STICK) UNSALTED BUTTER, MELTED

FILLING

3 CUPS CONFECTIONERS' SUGAR

½ CUP (1 STICK) UNSALTED BUTTER, MELTED AND SLIGHTLY COOLED

2 TEASPOONS PEPPERMINT EXTRACT

continued . . .

1　Line a 9-by-13-inch baking pan with aluminum foil, letting it slightly overhang the long sides of the pan. (These "handles" will make it easier to lift the cookie sheet from the pan.)

2　Prepare the crust. In a medium bowl, combine the cookie crumbs and butter, stirring and tossing with a fork to coat the crumbs with the butter. Transfer to the prepared pan, and pat evenly and firmly over the bottom. Refrigerate until firm, 20 to 30 minutes.

3　Prepare the filling. In a medium bowl, with an electric mixer, beat together the sugar, butter, and the peppermint and vanilla extracts until smooth. Beat in enough cream, if necessary, to make a smooth, easily spreadable buttercream. Add the food coloring, if using, mixing

continued . . .

. . . continued

1 TEASPOON VANILLA EXTRACT

1 TO 2 TABLESPOONS HEAVY CREAM, IF NEEDED

2 OR 3 DROPS GREEN FOOD COLORING (OPTIONAL)

TOPPING

9 OUNCES BITTERSWEET CHOCOLATE, CHOPPED, OR 1½ CUPS SEMISWEET CHOCOLATE CHIPS

¼ CUP HEAVY CREAM, OR AS NEEDED

well until the buttercream is a uniform light green. If you plan to decorate the tops of the cookies, set aside about 6 tablespoons of the buttercream to use for piping.

4 Spread the filling evenly over the cooled crust. Refrigerate until the buttercream is firm, 20 to 30 minutes.

5 Prepare the topping. Place the chocolate and ¼ cup cream in a microwave-safe bowl or in the top of a double boiler. Microwave at 80 percent power or heat over (not touching) barely simmering water, stirring occasionally, until melted and smooth (see page 67). The chocolate should pour easily from a spoon; if necessary, thin with additional cream. With an icing knife, spread the chocolate evenly over the buttercream filling.

6 Return the pan to the refrigerator until the topping is firm, about 2 hours. Using the foil as "handles," carefully lift the cookie sheet out of the pan onto a clean work surface. Using a sharp knife, cut the sheet into bars, wiping the knife clean with a damp kitchen towel after each cut.

7 If you have reserved some of the buttercream for decoration, spoon it into a pastry bag fitted with a small tip of choice, and pipe a design on each cookie. (We like to pipe a small leaf design on each one.) Or, thin the buttercream slightly with a little cream, and use a fork to drizzle it decoratively over the tops of the cookies.

8 Arrange the bars in a single layer on 1 or more plates, cover loosely with foil, and store in the refrigerator for up to 3 days. Let come to room temperature before serving. If they are too cold, the chocolate topping sometimes separates from the filling.

makes about
36
cookies

FUDGY
BROWNIE BITES

This recipe was a favorite of the late Irene Szczepaniak, whose daughter Diane graciously shared it with us. The brownies contain only a little flour, which makes them especially rich and fudgy.

COOKIE EXCHANGE TIP: These cookies are small but rich. They look nice artfully mounded on a gold metallic plate.

2 BARS (4 OUNCES EACH) GERMAN SWEET CHOCOLATE, CHOPPED

1 TABLESPOON UNSALTED BUTTER

¼ CUP ALL-PURPOSE FLOUR

¼ TEASPOON BAKING POWDER

¼ TEASPOON GROUND CINNAMON

⅛ TEASPOON SALT

2 LARGE EGGS

¾ CUP SUGAR

½ TEASPOON VANILLA EXTRACT

¾ CUP CHOPPED PECANS, PREFERABLY TOASTED (SEE PAGE 38)

1 Place the chocolate and butter in a microwave-safe bowl or in the top of a double boiler. Microwave at 50 percent power or heat over (not touching) barely simmering water, stirring occasionally, until melted and smooth (see page 67). Let cool.

2 Preheat the oven to 350°F. Lightly grease or spray cookie sheets.

3 In a small bowl, whisk together the flour, baking powder, cinnamon, and salt. Set aside.

4 In a large bowl, with an electric mixer, beat the eggs on high speed until foamy, about 2 minutes. Beat in the sugar, 2 tablespoons at a time. When all the sugar has been incorporated, beat the mixture on high speed until thickened and pale yellow, about 5 minutes. Beat in the cooled chocolate. On low speed, beat in the flour mixture and then the vanilla just until mixed. The dough will be soft, like a brownie batter. Stir in the pecans.

5 Drop the dough by rounded teaspoons onto the prepared cookie sheets, spacing them about 1½ inches apart.

6 Bake in the center of the oven until the tops feel set when very lightly touched with a fingertip, 8 to 10 minutes. Let cool on the cookie sheets for 2 to 3 minutes, then transfer to wire racks to cool completely.

MINI
DEVIL'S FOOD CUPCAKES WITH WHITE CHOCOLATE FILLING

makes 24 mini cupcakes

It is important not to overfill the muffin cups. If you use too much batter, the "cap" of the cupcake may separate from the base when you try to remove the cupcakes from the pan. Fill the cups two-thirds full, no more, to make nicely rounded cupcakes.

COOKIE EXCHANGE TIP: A little squiggle of white icing will remind people of their favorite childhood cupcake snacks—but these are all grown up.

⅓ CUP UNSWEETENED COCOA POWDER

¾ CUP BOILING WATER

1⅔ CUPS ALL-PURPOSE FLOUR

1 TEASPOON BAKING SODA

½ TEASPOON SALT

½ CUP (1 STICK) UNSALTED BUTTER, AT ROOM TEMPERATURE

1 CUP SUGAR

2 LARGE EGGS

1 TEASPOON VANILLA EXTRACT

1 Preheat the oven to 350°F. Line 24 mini muffin cups with paper or foil liners.

2 Place the cocoa in a heatproof measuring cup or bowl. Pour the boiling water over the cocoa and stir until a smooth paste forms. Let cool to room temperature.

3 In a medium bowl, sift together the flour, baking soda, and salt. Set aside.

4 In a large bowl, with an electric mixer, beat together the butter and sugar on medium speed until light, 2 to 3 minutes. Add the eggs, vanilla, and cooled cocoa mixture and beat just until mixed, about 2 minutes. On low speed, gradually add the flour mixture and beat just until fully blended. Spoon the batter into the prepared muffin cups, filling them two-thirds full.

5 Bake in the center of the oven until a cake tester inserted into the center of a cupcake comes out clean, 18 to 20 minutes. Let the cupcakes cool completely in the pan on a wire rack, then remove from the pan.

FILLING

3 OUNCES WHITE CHOCOLATE, CHOPPED, OR ½ CUP WHITE CHOCOLATE CHIPS

⅔ CUP HEAVY CREAM

GLAZE

6 OUNCES BITTERSWEET CHOCOLATE, CHOPPED, OR 1 CUP BITTERSWEET CHOCOLATE

1 CUP HEAVY CREAM

MELTED WHITE CHOCOLATE (SEE PAGE 67) OR WHITE DECORATOR ICING (OPTIONAL)

6 Prepare the filling. Place the white chocolate in a small bowl. In a small saucepan, scald the cream over medium heat. (Or, pour the cream into a glass measuring cup and scald in a microwave.) Pour the hot cream over the chocolate. Stir until the chocolate is melted and smooth. Refrigerate until cold.

7 Prepare the glaze. Place the bittersweet chocolate in a medium bowl. In a small saucepan, scald the cream over medium heat. (Or, pour the cream into a glass measuring cup and scald in a microwave.) Pour the hot cream over the chocolate and let stand for 30 seconds, then stir until the chocolate is melted and smooth. Let stand until thickened but still pourable, about 15 minutes.

8 When ready to fill and glaze the cooled cupcakes, remove the white chocolate mixture from the refrigerator. Using an electric mixer, beat on high speed until thickened and stiff peaks form, 3 to 5 minutes. Spoon into a pastry bag fitted with a medium round tip. Slip the tip of the pastry bag into the top of a cupcake, inserting it about halfway into the cake. Pipe the filling just until you feel some resistance and the top of the cupcake begins to bulge slightly. Scrape any excess filling off the top. Repeat to fill the remaining cupcakes the same way.

9 Swirl the top of each filled cupcake in the chocolate glaze until well coated, then place on the rack. If necessary, heat the glaze for a few seconds in the microwave on 20 percent power (low) to thin it.

10 Using a fork or spoon, drizzle the top of the each cupcake decoratively with melted white chocolate, or pipe a design on top with decorator icing. Let the cupcakes stand at cool room temperature until the glaze and decoration set.

CINNAMON CHIP–
CHOCOLATE CHIP COOKIES

Cinnamon-flavored chips, which are similar in shape and texture to chocolate chips, are available in many supermarkets around the holidays. The rest of the year, you can usually purchase them in baking supply or specialty foods stores or order them online. If you cannot find them, substitute white chocolate chips and increase the ground cinnamon to 1 teaspoon.

COOKIE EXCHANGE TIP: Package each batch of these cookies with a cinnamon stick to play up the cinnamon theme and to add a hint more cinnamon flavor to the cookies.

2 CUPS ALL-PURPOSE FLOUR

¼ CUP UNSWEETENED COCOA POWDER

½ TEASPOON GROUND CINNAMON, PLUS 1 TABLESPOON

1 TEASPOON BAKING SODA

½ TEASPOON SALT

1 CUP (2 STICKS) UNSALTED BUTTER, AT ROOM TEMPERATURE

1 CUP GRANULATED SUGAR

¾ CUP FIRMLY PACKED LIGHT BROWN SUGAR

2 LARGE EGGS

2 TEASPOONS VANILLA EXTRACT

1 CUP SEMISWEET CHOCOLATE CHIPS OR CHUNKS

1 CUP CINNAMON CHIPS

1   In a medium bowl, whisk together the flour, cocoa, the ½ teaspoon cinnamon, the baking soda, and salt. Set aside.

2   In a large bowl, with an electric mixer, beat the butter on medium speed until creamy, about 1 minute. Add ¾ cup of the granulated sugar and the brown sugar and beat until the mixture is light, about 2 minutes. Beat in the eggs, one at a time, beating well after each addition, and then beat in the vanilla. On low speed, gradually add the flour mixture and beat just until mixed. The dough will be soft. Stir in the chocolate chips and the cinnamon chips.

3   Cover the bowl and refrigerate until the dough is firm enough to be handled, about 30 minutes. Stir together the remaining ¼ cup granulated sugar and the 1 tablespoon cinnamon in a small bowl for rolling the cookies.

4 Preheat the oven to 375°F. Lightly grease or spray cookie sheets.

5 Pinch off pieces of the dough and roll between your palms into balls slightly larger than 1 inch. Roll each ball in the cinnamon sugar to coat evenly, then place on the prepared cookie sheets, spacing them about 2 inches apart.

6 Bake in the center of the oven until the tops are firm to the touch, 10 to 12 minutes. Let cool on the cookie sheets for 2 minutes, then transfer to wire racks to cool completely.

DARK
CHOCOLATE COOKIES STUDDED WITH
WHITE CHOCOLATE

For the best flavor, make sure to use real white chocolate chips—with a high cocoa butter content—not white baking chips (see page 66).

COOKIE EXCHANGE TIP: A little sprinkle of sea salt is an upscale touch that emphasizes the buttery white chocolate in these little cookies.

8 OUNCES SEMISWEET CHOCOLATE, CHOPPED

2 TABLESPOONS UNSALTED BUTTER

½ CUP PLUS 2 TABLESPOONS ALL-PURPOSE FLOUR

¼ TEASPOON BAKING POWDER

½ CUP FIRMLY PACKED DARK BROWN SUGAR

2 LARGE EGGS

1 TEASPOON VANILLA EXTRACT

½ CUP WHITE CHOCOLATE CHIPS

1 CUP CHOPPED WALNUTS OR PECANS, PREFERABLY TOASTED (SEE PAGE 38)

1 Preheat the oven to 350°F. Lightly grease or spray cookie sheets.

2 Place the semisweet chocolate and butter in a microwave-safe bowl or in the top pan of a double boiler. Microwave at 80 percent power or heat over (not touching) barely simmering water, stirring occasionally, until melted and smooth (see page 67). Set aside to cool slightly.

3 In a small bowl, sift together the flour and baking powder. Set aside.

4 In a large bowl, with an electric mixer, beat together the sugar, eggs, and vanilla until blended, about 2 minutes. Add the chocolate mixture. On low speed, gradually beat in the flour mixture just until mixed. Stir in the white chocolate chips and nuts. The dough will be soft and sticky.

5 Drop the dough by scant tablespoons onto the prepared cookie sheets, spacing them 1½ to 2 inches apart.

6 Bake in the center of the oven until the tops are firm to the touch, 8 to 10 minutes. Let the cookies cool completely on the cookie sheets on wire racks. They will firm up as they cool.

DOUBLE-CHOCOLATE
CHEWIES

makes about **32** cookies

This cookie is reminiscent of a meringue but not as fragile, making it easier to eat.

COOKIE EXCHANGE TIP: To up the decadence factor of these chewy cookies, use a dark, rich cocoa powder, such as Varlhona.

2 CUPS CONFECTIONERS' SUGAR

¾ CUP UNSWEETENED COCOA POWDER

¼ TEASPOON SALT

4 LARGE EGG WHITES

1¼ TEASPOONS VANILLA EXTRACT

1 CUP WHITE CHOCOLATE CHIPS OR SEMISWEET CHOCOLATE CHIPS

1 CUP CHOPPED WALNUTS, PECANS, OR MACADAMIA NUTS, PREFERABLY TOASTED (SEE PAGE 38)

1 Preheat the oven to 350°F. Line cookie sheets with parchment paper.

2 In a large bowl, sift together the confectioners' sugar, cocoa, and salt. With an electric mixer on high speed, beat the egg whites, one at a time, into the sugar mixture, then beat for about 4 minutes until a soft dough forms. Beat in the vanilla. Stir in the chocolate chips and nuts.

3 Drop the dough by heaping teaspoons onto the prepared cookie sheets, spacing them about 2 inches apart.

4 Bake in the center of the oven until the tops are just firm to the touch and have not begun to color, 10 to 12 minutes. Let the cookies cool completely on the cookie sheets on wire racks.

CHAPTER
4

COOKIE ORNAMENTS

This fanciful and imaginative group of cookie recipes will appeal to bakers who enjoy making crafts. The idea is to make and exchange cookies that can be displayed—strung along the mantel or over a doorway, hung in a window, lined up on a decorative shelf—or hung on the Christmas tree. Of course, you can also eat them—except for the Large Cinnamon Dough Angels (page 84), which are strictly ornamental—just after baking or after the tree comes down.

You can host an exchange to which each baker brings a batch of favorite cookie "ornaments," or you can host a crafts party: Bake the Large Cinnamon Dough Angels or Tuxedoed Gingerbread Polar Bears (page 80), put out icings, pastry bags and tips, food colorings, sprinkles and candies, and other decorating items, and let the partygoers decorate to their hearts' content.

When you make these ornaments, remember to provide a way to hang them. Use a ⅛-inch dowel or the narrow end of a chopstick to punch a hole in the top of each cookie before you bake the batch. If the holes have partly closed up during baking, punch them again while the cookies are still warm.

Larger cookies, such as the teddy bears or the angels, are meant to be exchanged one for one. Other cookies, like the Candy Cane Cookies (page 82), should be exchanged in batches, because they look best when several of them are hanging on a Christmas tree. At the party, display samples of the partygoers' cookie ornaments on the host's tree so everyone can see how attractive they are.

TUXEDOED GINGERBREAD

POLAR BEARS

makes about
17
bears

Use either a sitting or standing teddy bear cutter, or you can make tuxedoed gingerbread men instead of bears. These fancy-dressed cookies also taste good made with Basic Butter Cookies (page 150) or Cream Cheese Sugar Cookies (page 154) dough instead of gingerbread.

COOKIE EXCHANGE TIP: A white tray decorated with a red or black bow will give these elegant polar bears the setting they deserve. For exchanging, wrap each bear in clear cellophane and tie with a bright red ribbon.

BASIC GINGERBREAD (PAGE 50)

POURED FONDANT ICING (PAGE 15)

CHOCOLATE POURED FONDANT ICING (PAGE 15)

BLACK FOOD COLORING, OR A BLEND OF 1 PART EACH RED, BLUE, AND YELLOW FOOD COLORING

RED DECORATOR ICING

1 Make the gingerbread dough and refrigerate as directed.

2 Preheat the oven to 350°F. Lightly grease or spray cookie sheets.

3 Place 1 dough disk on a lightly floured pastry cloth or board, and roll out ¼ inch thick. Using a 4½- to 5-inch teddy bear cookie cutter, cut out cookies. Using a large spatula, carefully transfer the cookies to the prepared cookie sheets, spacing them about 1½ inches apart. Repeat with the second dough disk. Combine the scraps, reroll, and cut out more cookies.

4 Bake in the center of the oven until set on top and golden on the bottom, 12 to 15 minutes. Let cool on the cookie sheets for 2 minutes, then transfer to wire racks to cool completely.

5 Using an icing spatula, spread the white fondant icing evenly over each bear. Let stand until the icing is set, at least 30 minutes.

6   Add black food coloring to the chocolate fondant to make black icing. With a small brush, spread or dab the black icing over the bear to resemble a tuxedo, leaving the "shirt" area white and leaving white lines to suggest lapels. Thin the icing with a little corn syrup if it's too thick to brush easily.

7   Spoon some of the black icing into a pastry bag fitted with a small round tip (or, use a black decorating pen). Pipe 4 short lines on each foot and hand to resemble claws. Pipe on a mouth, nose, and eyes, and outline the ears. Using red decorator icing, pipe or paint on a red bowtie.

8   Let the polar bears stand until the icing is set.

makes
42
cookies

CANDY CANE COOKIES

Be careful when you serve these. They are cute enough to tempt Santa away from his appointed rounds.

COOKIE EXCHANGE TIP: To use these cookies as tree ornaments, gently tie a red or white ribbon around the handle of the cane, creating a 2- to 3-inch loop that will easily slip onto the branch of the tree. Or, make a hole in the handle of the cane before baking (see page 79), and then thread the ribbon through the hole.

1 CUP (2 STICKS) UNSALTED BUTTER, AT ROOM TEMPERATURE

1 CUP CONFECTIONERS' SUGAR

1 LARGE EGG

1 TEASPOON ALMOND EXTRACT

½ TEASPOON SALT

2½ CUPS ALL-PURPOSE FLOUR

½ TEASPOON RED FOOD COLORING

¾ CUP WHITE DECORATING SUGAR OR GRANULATED SUGAR

1   Preheat the oven to 375°F. Have ready ungreased nonstick cookie sheets.

2   In a large bowl, with an electric mixer, beat together the butter and confectioners' sugar until light, 2 to 3 minutes. Beat in the egg, almond extract, and salt. On low speed, gradually beat in the flour until a medium-firm dough forms.

3   Divide the dough in half. Beat the red food coloring into half of the dough. Blend until the color is evenly mixed throughout the dough.

4   Pinch off 1 teaspoon of the red dough. Roll between your palms to form a 4-inch-long rope. Pinch off 1 teaspoon of the plain dough and form into a 4-inch-long rope. Press the ropes to each other at one end and then twist them together to resemble a striped cane. Shape one end into a hook. Repeat with the remaining dough. As the cookies are shaped, arrange them on the cookie sheets, spacing them about ⅛ inch apart.

5   Bake in the center of the oven until just firm when lightly pressed with a fingertip, 8 to 10 minutes. Remove from the oven and sprinkle with the decorating sugar while still hot. Let cool on the cookie sheets for 2 minutes, then transfer the cookies to wire racks to cool completely.

LARGE CINNAMON DOUGH
ANGELS

makes
8
angels

Normally, cinnamon dough, which makes sweet-smelling ornaments, contains nearly all cinnamon (and often white school glue) and is not edible. Our version is edible, in theory at least. In reality, these angels are too pretty to eat. We dry them in a 200°F oven to save time, but you could just leave them in a warm spot overnight to dry.

COOKIE EXCHANGE TIP: These hand-cut angels will impress fellow cookie exchangers. But if time is short or you need more cookies to exchange, cut out the dough with a large angel-shaped cookie cutter.

1 CUP SMOOTH APPLESAUCE

⅔ CUP GROUND CINNAMON

1 LARGE EGG WHITE

2¼ TO 2½ CUPS ALL-PURPOSE FLOUR

1 EGG BEATEN WITH 1 TEASPOON WATER

FOR DECORATING

ROYAL ICING (PAGE 14)

DECORATING SUGARS OR FOOD COLORINGS IN GOLD OR SILVER AND RED OR OTHER COLOR

DECORATING PENS

1 In a medium bowl, stir together the applesauce, cinnamon, and egg white. Stir in 2¼ cups of the flour. Turn the dough out onto a floured board and knead it until it is stiff, pliable, and no longer sticky, about 2 minutes. It should be the consistency of modeling dough. Knead in up to ¼ cup additional flour to achieve the correct consistency. If the dough is too stiff, add a bit of water, a teaspoon at a time.

2 Preheat the oven to 200°F. Have ready nonstick cookie sheets or line regular cookie sheets with parchment paper or waxed paper.

3 Place the dough on a lightly floured pastry cloth or board, and roll out into a rectangle about ¼ inch thick and at least 12 inches long and 5 inches wide. Cut 2 rectangles from the dough, each 2⅛ inches wide by 12 inches long. With a sharp knife, cut each rectangle crosswise at 3-inch intervals to make 4 rectangles each 2⅛ inches by 3 inches. Cut through each rectangle on the diagonal, leaving about ⅛ inch uncut at one end, to make 2 triangles that are attached to each other. These will be the wings. You should have 8 sets of wings.

continued . . .

. . . *continued*

4 Reroll the dough scraps to ³⁄₁₆ inch thick. Cut 8 rectangles each 1½ inches wide by 5 inches long, for the angel bodies. Reroll the dough scraps ⅛ inch thick and cut 8 circles, each 1¼ inches in diameter, for the angel heads. (If you do not have a cutter this size, use a bottle lid or the top of the empty cinnamon bottle.) Cut another 8 circles, each 2 inches in diameter, for the halos. (Halos are nice, but optional.) Gather and reroll the scraps as necessary.

5 Place a pair of the triangles, long side and tips at the top, on a cookie sheet. Where the triangles are attached, brush with a little of the egg-water mixture. Place 1 of the narrow rectangles on top of the wings, with the top of the rectangle even at the point at which the triangles are attached. If you like, fan out the bottom of the rectangle slightly to resemble a skirt. Brush the top edge of the rectangle with a bit of the egg-water mixture and place 1 of the 2-inch circles at the top for a halo. Lightly pinch the dough where the halo, wings, and body meet, securing them together. Dab a little egg-water mixture on the center of the halo. Set an angel head on the halo, overlapping it slightly over the angel's body. Repeat with the remaining dough pieces. You will be able to fit only 3 or 4 angels on a cookie sheet. Punch a hole at the top of each halo (page 79), for threading a ribbon if you choose to hang the finished angels.

6   Place in the center of the oven and heat for 45 minutes. Using a wide spatula, carefully transfer the angels directly to the oven rack and continue baking until hard and dry, 30 to 45 minutes longer. Carefully transfer to wire racks to cool completely.

7   To decorate, using an icing spatula or spoon, spread the icing thinly over each angel, covering the wings, body, head, and halo. While the icing is wet, sprinkle it with colored sugars, using gold or silver for the wings and halo, and red or a color of your choice for the body. When the icing is set, shake off the excess sugar. Or, spoon the icing into a pastry bag fitted with a round tip and pipe a line of the icing about ⅛ inch in from the edge of angel, outlining the angel completely. Or, spread or pipe the icing and let it dry, then paint it with food coloring in different colors, using a clean artist's paintbrush.

8   If any of the angels come apart, repair them by gluing the pieces together with a little of the icing.

HAND-PAINTED
XMAS COOKIE RINGS

makes
40
cookies

You can use a doughnut cutter to cut out these tree ornaments. Or, use a large round cookie cutter to cut out each cookie, then a smaller cutter (1 to 1½ inches in diameter) to cut the hole in the center.

COOKIE EXCHANGE TIP: For an artistic touch, brush the cookie rings with glaze, let the glaze dry, and then paint and decorate the cookie. The light undercoat of color nicely reflects the painted design.

BASIC BUTTER COOKIES DOUGH
(PAGE 150)

PAINT GLAZE

½ CUP SIFTED CONFECTIONERS' SUGAR

2 TO 3 TABLESPOONS HEAVY CREAM OR MILK, AS NEEDED

¼ TEASPOON VANILLA, ORANGE, OR LEMON EXTRACT

GEL OR PASTE FOOD COLORING IN 1 OR MORE COLORS

1 Make the butter cookies dough and refrigerate as directed.

2 Preheat the oven to 350°F. Have ready ungreased cookie sheets.

3 Divide the chilled dough in half. Place half of the dough on a lightly floured pastry cloth or board, and roll out ¼ inch thick. Using a 3-inch doughnut cutter, cut out cookies. (Or, cut out the cookies with a 3-inch round cookie cutter, and then cut out the center of the cookie with a 1- to 1½-inch round cutter.) Using a spatula, transfer the rings to the cookie sheets, spacing them about 1½ inches apart. Repeat with the second half of the dough. Combine the scraps, reroll, and cut out more cookies.

4 Bake in the center of the oven until faintly golden, 8 to 10 minutes. Let cool on the cookie sheets for 2 minutes, then transfer the cookies to wire racks and let cool completely.

continued...

. . . *continued*

5   Prepare the glaze. Sift the sugar into a small bowl. Whisk in 2 table-
    spoons cream and the vanilla until smooth, then whisk in the food
    coloring until evenly colored. The glaze will be thin. (Or, you can
    use a food processor to make the glaze, omitting the sifting and
    processing until smooth, and then whisking in the food coloring.)
    To make different colors, spoon some of the plain glaze into the cups
    of a muffin tin or the compartments of an ice-cube tray, and mix a
    different color into each batch.

6   Using a soft pastry brush or a wide, soft artist's paintbrush, brush the
    cookie rings with the glaze, painting designs as you like. Let the glaze
    set before serving or hanging the cookies. When the glaze is dry, you
    can paint more designs on the cookies with food coloring.

MINT MERINGUE WREATHS

makes about **36** cookies

If you want to tint the cookies green, mix a few drops of green food coloring into the batter and mix until combined. You can also decorate the wreaths before baking with mini chocolate chips or mini red candies to represent lights.

COOKIE EXCHANGE TIP: Loop a thin, red ribbon through each wreath for hanging it on a tree.

6 LARGE EGG WHITES, AT ROOM TEMPERATURE

½ TEASPOON CREAM OF TARTAR

1 CUP SUGAR

¼ CUP HARD MINT CANDIES, CRUSHED, OR ½ TEASPOON MINT EXTRACT

1 Preheat the oven to 225°F. Line cookie sheets with aluminum foil or parchment paper. If using parchment, use a pencil to draw 2⅛-inch circles on the parchment, about 1 inch apart. Place the parchment on the cookie sheets, penciled side down. If using foil, line the sheets with the foil, then use a wooden spoon handle or chopstick to impress 2⅛-inch circles in the foil.

2 In a large bowl, with an electric mixer, beat the egg whites on high speed until foamy. Beat in the cream of tartar. With the mixer still on high speed, add the sugar in a slow, steady stream, and continue to beat until stiff, glossy peaks form, 2 to 3 minutes. Do not overbeat. Fold in the candies with a rubber spatula.

3 Spoon half of the meringue into pastry bag fitted with a large open star tip. Keep the remaining meringue covered with plastic wrap.

4 Pipe the meringue decoratively within the circles on the prepared cookie sheets, creating a wreath design in each circle. Repeat with the remaining meringue to make more wreaths.

5 Bake in the center of the oven until firm and dry, about 1 hour. Turn off the oven and leave the meringues in the oven overnight.

6 Carefully peel the foil from the wreaths.

MERINGUE
SNOWFLAKES

makes
12
large
cookies

Like all meringues, these should be made on a dry day. You can use any snow-flake pattern you wish (you can find plenty of paper snowflake patterns online). If you're ambitious or have several people making these, you can make each snowflake different. This is a recipe for bakers who have mastered piping.

COOKIE EXCHANGE TIP: These meringue treats are fragile, so transport them care-fully. They look good on a silver platter sprinkled with white and silver decorating sugars. To hang the snowflakes, thread a narrow silver or white ribbon through an opening in the design and tie to make a loop.

3 LARGE EGG WHITES, AT ROOM TEMPERATURE

¼ TEASPOON CREAM OF TARTAR

1 CUP GRANULATED SUGAR

½ TEASPOON CLEAR EXTRACT OR FLAVORING, SUCH AS VANILLA, PEPPERMINT, ALMOND, LEMON, OR ORANGE

WHITE DECORATING OR GRANULATED SUGAR

EDIBLE WHITE GLITTER (OPTIONAL)

1   First, create snowflake designs: Use your own paper snowflake designs cut from dark paper, or use printed snowflake designs from other sources (print them in black or another dark color so they show through the baking parchment). For best results, use patterns about 5 inches in diameter, with designs that are not too intricate.

2   Preheat the oven to 200°F. Place the snowflake designs on cookie sheets, spacing them at least 1 inch apart. Lay a sheet of parchment paper or waxed paper over the designs, pressing it smooth and flat. (It may help to lightly dampen the bottom edges of the parchment paper so the paper will adhere to the pan.)

3   In a large bowl, with an electric mixer, beat the egg whites on high speed until foamy. Beat in the cream of tartar. With the mixer still on high speed, add the granulated sugar in a slow, steady stream, and continue to beat until stiff, glossy peaks form, 2 to 3 minutes. Do not overbeat. Beat in the extract.

continued . . .

. . . continued

4 Spoon half of the meringue into a pastry bag fitted with a ⅜-inch round or open star tip. Keep the remaining meringue covered with plastic wrap.

5 Pipe the meringue onto the prepared cookie sheets, following the design of the snowflake patterns. Sprinkle with sugar and glitter, if using. Repeat with the remaining meringue to make more snowflakes.

6 Bake in the center of the oven until firm, about 30 minutes. Turn off the oven and leave the meringues in the oven until dry and crisp, at least 3 hours or up to overnight.

7 Carefully peel the parchment from the snowflakes.

SUGAR PRETZELS

makes
15
cookies

Use decorating sugar to mimic the salt on savory pretzels.

COOKIE EXCHANGE TIP: To use the pretzels as tree ornaments, thread a narrow fabric ribbon with a pretty design through the top part of each pretzel and tie it to make a loop.

½ CUP (1 STICK) UNSALTED BUTTER, AT ROOM TEMPERATURE

¼ CUP GRANULATED SUGAR

1 LARGE EGG

1¼ TEASPOONS VANILLA EXTRACT

1½ CUPS ALL-PURPOSE FLOUR

1 LARGE EGG WHITE, LIGHTLY BEATEN

COARSE WHITE OR RED DECORATING SUGAR FOR SPRINKLING

1 In a large bowl, with an electric mixer, beat together the butter and granulated sugar on medium speed until light, 2 to 3 minutes. Beat in the egg and vanilla. On low speed, gradually beat in the flour just until mixed and a soft dough forms.

2 Gather the dough into a ball and wrap with plastic wrap. Refrigerate until firm, 1 to 2 hours.

3 Lightly grease or spray cookie sheets. Pinch off 3 tablespoons of the dough. Using your palms, roll on a lightly floured work surface into a 9-inch-long rope. Loop the ends of the rope around each other and then gently press the ends onto the circle, forming a pretzel shape. Place the cookie on a prepared cookie sheet. Repeat until you have made 15 cookies total, spacing them about 2 inches apart. Cover lightly with plastic wrap and refrigerate for 45 minutes.

4 Preheat the oven to 375°F. Using a pastry brush, coat the cookies with the egg white. Sprinkle with the decorating sugar.

5 Bake in the center of the oven until just firm when lightly touched with a fingertip, 12 to 14 minutes. Let cool on the cookie sheets for 3 to 4 minutes, then transfer to wire racks to cool completely.

STAINED-GLASS ORNAMENTS

makes
30
cookies

Use fruit-flavored Life Savers, sour balls, or similar hard candies for the "stained glass." It is fun to make your own design for the ornaments. For example, if you want to make a holly leaf or a dove, draw the shape on a piece of cardboard—about 3 inches in diameter is a good size—and cut it out. Edge the gingerbread strips around the design on the cookie sheet. Continue until all the gingerbread has been used.

To crush the candies, use a food processor or place the candies between 2 pieces of waxed paper and crush with a rolling pin.

COOKIE EXCHANGE TIP: To make this cookie into a tree ornament, attach a loop made from the dough to the top of the cookie before baking. After the cookie is baked, thread a piece of ribbon through the loop and tie the ribbon in a bow. To make these ornaments at a party, prepare the cardboard patterns in advance.

3 CUPS ALL-PURPOSE FLOUR

1 TEASPOON BAKING SODA

¼ TEASPOON SALT

¾ TEASPOON GROUND CINNAMON

½ TEASPOON GROUND GINGER

⅛ TEASPOON GROUND NUTMEG

3 TABLESPOONS UNSALTED BUTTER, AT ROOM TEMPERATURE

½ CUP FIRMLY PACKED DARK BROWN SUGAR

¾ CUP UNSULFURED MOLASSES

⅓ CUP WATER

6 OUNCES TRANSLUCENT HARD CANDIES IN COLORS OF CHOICE, CRUSHED

1 In a large bowl, whisk together the flour, baking soda, salt, cinnamon, ginger, and nutmeg. Set aside.

2 In a large bowl, with an electric mixer, beat the butter on medium speed until creamy. Add the sugar and molasses and beat for 2 minutes. Beat in the water. On low speed, beat in the flour mixture until a soft dough forms.

3 Gather the dough into a ball and wrap in plastic wrap. Refrigerate until firm, at least 1 hour or up to overnight.

4 Preheat the oven to 350°F. Line cookie sheets with aluminum foil.

continued . . .

. . . *continued*

5   Divide the dough into thirds. Divide each third into 10 equal pieces. Using your palms, roll each piece on a lightly floured work surface into a rope ¼ to ½ inch in diameter. Gently trace the design of your choice onto the prepared cookie sheets (a wooden spoon handle or chopstick works well for tracing on foil). Outline each design with a rope of dough, pressing the ends together to seal securely.

6   Sprinkle the inside of each design with the crushed candies, dividing the candies evenly among the outlined designs and creating an even layer.

7   Bake in the center of the oven or until the edges of the cookies are golden and the candy has melted, 6 to 9 minutes. Let the cookies cool on the cookie sheets on wire racks until the candy hardens, about 5 minutes. Gently peel away the foil from the cookies and transfer to the racks to cool completely.

RED-NOSED
RUDOLPH COOKIES

makes
36
cookies

To get broken pieces that are suitable as antlers, expect to waste a few pretzels on this. For an easier, but not as authentic-looking, set of antlers, use the mini pretzels whole, placing them at an angle on each side of the top of the head.

COOKIE EXCHANGE TIP: These reindeer faces are adorable displayed in a wicker sleigh. Or, hang them on the tree: Make a hole in the top of each cookie (see page 79), and tie a bright red ribbon through the baked cookie.

BASIC GINGERBREAD (PAGE 50)

72 BROWN M&M'S OR CHOCOLATE CHIPS

18 RED CANDIED CHERRIES OR DRAINED RED MARASCHINO CHERRIES, CUT IN HALF

50 TO 60 MINI PRETZEL TWISTS

1 Make the gingerbread dough as directed.

2 On a lightly floured board, shape the dough into a triangular log about 10 inches long. (The dough may be easier to work with if you chill it for 30 minutes before you shape it.) Refrigerate until firm, at least several hours or up to overnight.

3 Preheat the oven to 350°F. Lightly grease or spray cookie sheets.

4 Cut the log into slices ¼ inch thick. Place on the prepared cookie sheets, spacing them at least 1½ inches apart. Use your fingers to shape the triangles a bit to resemble reindeer faces, pulling the dough into 2 knobs on the short side of the triangle to suggest "ears."

5 Set 2 M&M's or chocolate chips on each cookie to make the eyes, and place a cherry half, cut side down, at the point of each cookie to make a nose. Carefully break the pretzels into antlerlike pieces, and insert 2 antlers at the top of each cookie.

6 Bake in the center of the oven until set to the touch but not browned, 8 to 10 minutes. Let cool on the cookie sheets for 2 minutes, then transfer to wire racks to cool completely.

PART 3

COOKIES BY TECHNIQUE

CHAPTER 1:
DROP COOKIES 102
Amaretti 104
Poinsettia Cookies 105
Russian Walnut Tea Cakes 106
Orange-Scented Snowballs 108
Lace Cookies 109
Saint Nicholas Cookies 110
Lemon-Iced Cookies 112
Small Black and Whites 115
Green Tea–Lemon Wafers 117
Candied-Fruit Florentines 118
Macaroons with Almond Paste 120
Kris Kringle Cookies 121
Oatmeal Brickle Nuggets 122
Chocolate Mincemeat Jumbles 124
Chocolate-Orange Cookies 125

CHAPTER 2:
BARS AND SQUARES 126
Date-Filled Bars 128
Raspberry Linzer Squares 130
Croatian Jam-Filled Walnut
   Meringue Bars 132
Five-Layer Bars 133
Apricot Bars 135
Old-Fashioned Apple Squares 137
Lemon Bars with a
   Coconut Crust 138
Italian Tricolor Cookies 140
Greek Custard Bars 142
Chocolate-Topped Pecan Bars 144
Crispy Cereal Bars with
   Chocolate on Top 145
Toffee Squares 146

CHAPTER 3: ROLLED AND
CUTOUT COOKIES 148
Basic Butter Cookies 150
Santa Grahams 151
Christmas Cutout Cookies 152
Cream Cheese Sugar Cookies
   with *Dulce de Leche* 154
German Streusel Cookies 158
Sand Tarts 160
Holiday Cinnamon Stars 161
Chocolate Rice Cereal
   Rocking Horses 162
Bizcochitos 163

CHAPTER 4: SLICE-AND-
BAKE COOKIES 164
Glacé Cherry Holiday Slices 166
Chocolate-Cherry Ribbon Cookies . . 168
Pistachio and Cranberry Biscotti . . . 171
Seedy, Nutty Little Slices 173
Checkerboard Cookies 174
Molasses Cookies with
   Butter-Nut Topping 176
Mincemeat and Lemon Cookies 178
Lime-Pistachio Thins 179

CHAPTER 5:
FILLED COOKIES 180
Vanilla Sandwich Cookies 182
Chocolate Sandwich Cookies with
   Marshmallow-Mint Filling 183
Soft Sandwich Cookies 185
Two-Bite Oatmeal Sandwich Cookies
   with Nutella Filling 186
Kolacky 189
Bear Paws 191
Swedish Thumbprint Cookies 192

Pine Nut Thumbprint Cookies
   with Fig Jam 194
Chocolate Peanut Butter Cups 197
Cinnamon-Nut Horns 199
Rolled Coconut-Strawberry
   Cookies 200
Chocolate-Nut Crescents 202

CHAPTER 6: MOLDED AND
STAMPED COOKIES 204
Five-Spice Shortbread 206
Chocolate-Dipped Shortbread 207
Ginger Shortbread 210
Finnish Almond Logs 211
Christmas Mice Cookies 212
Molded Dutch Spice Cookies 214
Almond Crescents Dipped in
   White Chocolate 216
Almond Tuiles 217
Mini Eggnog Madeleines 218
Scandinavian Stamp Cookies 220
Kringles 221
Italian Twisted Wreath Cookies . . . 222
Brandy Snaps 224
Turtles 226
Bowknots 228
Honey–Pine Nut Crescents 230
Cereal Wreath Treats 231

CHAPTER 7: PRESSED AND
PIPED COOKIES 232
Spritz Christmas Trees
   and Wreaths 234
Mocha Tweed Ribbons 236
Chai Meringues 237
Spicy Cinnamon Meringues 238
Twinkling Little Stars 289

CHAPTER
I

DROP COOKIES

Drop cookies radiate a homey appeal. Unlike the uniform, machine-made cookies you find in the grocery store, no two homemade drop cookies are alike. They are also among the easiest cookies to make from scratch. Most recipes call for little or no chilling, shaping, or filling. Just mix up the dough, drop it from a spoon or roll it into balls, and bake. Here are four tips to smooth your time in the kitchen:

1. Some recipes for drop cookies call for rolling the dough into balls to create uniformly round cookies. For a better presentation at a cookie exchange, you can use this technique with nearly any drop cookie, as long as the dough is firm enough (you can even refrigerate soft doughs, such as chocolate chip cookie dough, to make them firm enough for rolling). Shaping the dough into balls also produces baked cookies with more heft.

2. The typical way to shape the dough is by rolling it between your palms. For the most uniform cookies, use cookie scoops or meatball scoops, which look like ice cream scoops but are smaller. If you are making larger cookies, ice cream scoops work, too.

3. Refrigerate sticky dough, such as the dough for chocolate chip cookies, until it is easy to handle. Usually it needs to chill for no more than about 30 minutes.

4. Pay attention to the size specified in the recipe if you want to get the same yield the recipe indicates. A 1-inch ball of dough may be smaller than you think it is.

AMARETTI

These famous, flourless Italian cookies are like crunchy macaroons. For even better flavor, toast the almonds before you grind them.

COOKIE EXCHANGE TIP: Tell Santa to try these cookies with a cup of his favorite espresso—or with a small glass of amaretto, if he is feeling very Italian.

1¼ CUPS GROUND ALMONDS

½ CUP GRANULATED SUGAR

1 TABLESPOON UNSWEETENED COCOA POWDER

2 TABLESPOONS CONFECTIONERS' SUGAR

2 LARGE EGG WHITES

⅛ TEASPOON CREAM OF TARTAR

1 TEASPOON ALMOND EXTRACT

24 SLIVERED BLANCHED ALMONDS FOR GARNISH

1 Preheat the oven to 325°F. Lightly spray nonstick cookie sheets.

2 In a medium bowl, stir together the ground almonds, ¼ cup of the granulated sugar, the cocoa powder, and the confectioners' sugar. Set aside.

3 In a large bowl, with an electric mixer, beat the egg whites on high speed until soft peaks form. Beat in the remaining ¼ cup granulated sugar, a tablespoon at a time, until all the sugar has been added. Then beat in the almond mixture, cream of tartar, and almond extract until a medium-soft dough forms.

4 Drop cookies from a teaspoon in a rounded shape onto the prepared cookie sheets, spacing them about 2 inches apart. (Or, use a pastry bag fitted with a ½-inch round or star tip and pipe the cookies about 1½ inches wide and about 2 inches apart on the prepared cookie sheets.) Place a slivered almond on top of each cookie.

5 Bake in the center of the oven until crisp and the bottoms are golden, 13 to 15 minutes. Let cool on the cookie sheets until they firm up, about 3 minutes, then transfer to wire racks to cool completely.

POINSETTIA COOKIES

makes
48
cookies

Red candied cherries work best, but if you cannot find them, you can substitute red maraschino cherries. Be sure to drain them well.

COOKIE EXCHANGE TIP: The jewel-like poinsettia design on the top makes this cookie a gem. Children and adults will come back for more. As a bonus, this cookie is easy to make and transport.

3 CUPS ALL-PURPOSE FLOUR

½ TEASPOON SALT

1 CUP (2 STICKS) UNSALTED BUTTER, AT ROOM TEMPERATURE

2 CUPS CONFECTIONERS' SUGAR

2 LARGE EGGS

1½ TEASPOONS VANILLA EXTRACT

1 CUP SWEETENED SHREDDED COCONUT

GRANULATED SUGAR FOR DIPPING

1¼ CUPS BUTTERSCOTCH CHIPS

½ CUP CANDIED RED CHERRIES, CUT IN HALF AND EACH HALF CUT INTO 4 WEDGES

1 In a medium bowl, whisk together the flour and salt. Set aside.

2 In a large bowl, with an electric mixer, beat together the butter and confectioners' sugar on medium speed until light, 2 to 3 minutes. Beat in the eggs, one at a time, beating after each addition, and then beat in the vanilla. Add the flour mixture and beat until combined. Stir in the coconut and ¾ cup of the butterscotch chips until a medium-soft dough forms.

3 Gather the dough into a ball and wrap in plastic wrap. Refrigerate until firm, about 2 hours.

4 Preheat the oven to 375°F. Have ready ungreased nonstick cookie sheets.

5 Pinch off pieces of the dough and roll between your palms into 1-inch balls. Place on the cookie sheets, spacing them about 1½ inches apart. Lightly flatten the balls with the bottom of a drinking glass dipped in granulated sugar. Press a butterscotch chip in the center of each cookie. Arrange 5 cherry wedges in a circle around the butterscotch chip, radiating from the center like petals.

6 Bake in the center of the oven until the tops are set to the touch and the bottoms are golden around the edges, 10 to 12 minutes. Let cool on the cookie sheets for 2 minutes, then transfer to wire racks to cool completely.

RUSSIAN
WALNUT TEA CAKES

Sift the sugar for rolling so it doesn't clump up. The cookies are fragile, so roll them gently in the sugar.

COOKIE EXCHANGE TIP: This is a safe choice for any cookie exchange. Everyone likes these melt-in-the-mouth tea cakes, and they are easy to make. Arrange them on a doily-lined silver plate.

1 CUP (2 STICKS) UNSALTED BUTTER, AT ROOM TEMPERATURE

½ CUP CONFECTIONERS' SUGAR, PLUS 1 CUP SIFTED FOR ROLLING

¼ TEASPOON GROUND CINNAMON

¼ TEASPOON SALT

2¼ CUPS ALL-PURPOSE FLOUR

1 CUP GROUND WALNUTS, PREFERABLY TOASTED (SEE PAGE 38)

1   Preheat the oven to 350°F. Have ready ungreased cookie sheets.

2   In a large bowl, with an electric mixer, beat together the butter, the ½ cup confectioners' sugar, the cinnamon, and salt on medium speed until smooth and creamy, about 2 minutes. On low speed, gradually beat in the flour and then the nuts just until mixed. The dough will be stiff and somewhat crumbly.

3   Pinch off pieces of the dough and roll between your palms into 1-inch balls. Place on the cookie sheets, spacing them about 1⅛ inches apart.

4   Bake in the center of the oven until the tops are set to the touch and the bottoms are lightly golden, about 10 minutes. Let the cookies cool on the cookie sheets until they are still warm but are firm enough to handle without crumbling.

5   Spread the 1 cup sifted confectioners' sugar on a plate. Roll the warm cookies in the sugar, coating them evenly. Set on wire racks to cool completely. When the cookies have cooled, roll them again lightly in the sugar.

ORANGE-SCENTED
SNOWBALLS

makes
40
cookies

These are rich and melt-in-the-mouth tender, just like Russian tea cakes (page 106), but they are also an ideal choice for anyone who doesn't like—or can't eat—nuts.

COOKIE EXCHANGE TIP: For an attractive presentation, dust the serving plate with sifted confectioners' sugar, and scatter strips of orange peel here and there on the sugar. Mound the cookies on the plate and dust with more confectioners' sugar.

1 CUP (2 STICKS) UNSALTED BUTTER, AT ROOM TEMPERATURE

½ CUP CONFECTIONERS' SUGAR, PLUS ¾ CUP SIFTED FOR ROLLING

½ TEASPOON ORANGE EXTRACT, OR 2 TEASPOONS FINELY GRATED ORANGE ZEST

⅛ TEASPOON SALT

2 CUPS ALL-PURPOSE FLOUR

1 Preheat the oven to 350°F. Have ready ungreased baking sheets.

2 In a large bowl, with an electric mixer, beat together the butter, the ½ cup sugar, the orange extract, and salt until smooth and creamy, about 2 minutes. On low speed, beat in the flour just until mixed. The dough will be medium-stiff.

3 Pinch off pieces of the dough and roll between your palms into 1-inch balls. Place on the cookie sheets, spacing them about 1½ inches apart.

4 Bake in the center of the oven until the tops are set to the touch and the bottoms are lightly golden, 10 to 12 minutes. Let the cookies cool on the cookie sheets until they are still warm but are firm enough to handle without crumbling.

5 Spread the ¾ cup sifted confectioners' sugar on a plate. Roll the warm cookies in the sugar, coating them evenly. Set on wire racks to cool completely. When the cookies have cooled, roll them again lightly in the sugar.

LACE COOKIES

makes **32** cookies

These crisp cookies are thin and fragile, so make sure they are completely cooled before attempting to move them.

COOKIE EXCHANGE TIP: Named for their thin, lacy appearance, these cookies look great arranged on a serving plate lined with a large paper doily. They are crisp and fragile, so handle them gently.

4 TABLESPOONS (½ STICK) UNSALTED BUTTER OR MARGARINE

1 CUP PLUS 2 TABLESPOONS OLD-FASHIONED ROLLED OATS

½ CUP PLUS 2 TABLESPOONS SUGAR

1 LARGE EGG

1 TABLESPOON ALL-PURPOSE FLOUR

1 TEASPOON BAKING POWDER

½ CUP CHOPPED PECANS OR WALNUTS, PREFERABLY TOASTED (SEE PAGE 38)

1 Preheat the oven to 350°F. Line cookie sheets with aluminum foil or parchment paper.

2 In a small, heavy saucepan, melt the butter over low heat. Remove from the heat and stir in the oats, sugar, egg, flour, and baking powder, mixing well. Stir in the nuts.

3 Drop by teaspoons onto the prepared cookie sheets, spacing them at least 2 inches apart.

4 Bake in the center of the oven until still slightly soft in the center and golden around the edges, about 10 minutes. Let cool completely on the cookie sheets on wire racks. The cookies will crisp up as they cool. Carefully peel the cooled cookies from the foil.

SAINT NICHOLAS COOKIES

makes about 60 cookies

Barbara found these Dutch cookies in her mother's cookie collection. They are similar to the *speculaas* on page 214, but they contain fruit and are not molded. Candied (glacé) lemon peel and pineapple are especially nice in these mildly spiced cookies.

COOKIE EXCHANGE TIP: It is tempting to skip the frosting on the cookie, but please don't. It not only makes them more attractive for an exchange, but also helps to round out the warm, spicy flavor notes.

4 CUPS CAKE FLOUR

1 TEASPOON BAKING SODA

1 TEASPOON GROUND CINNAMON

½ TEASPOON GROUND NUTMEG

½ TEASPOON GROUND CLOVES

½ TEASPOON SALT

1 CUP (2 STICKS) UNSALTED BUTTER, AT ROOM TEMPERATURE

1½ CUPS CONFECTIONERS' SUGAR

3 LARGE EGGS

1 CUP FINELY CHOPPED CANDIED CITRUS PEELS AND/OR FRUITS OF CHOICE

1 CUP FINELY CHOPPED WALNUTS, PECANS, ALMONDS, OR HAZELNUTS, PREFERABLY TOASTED (SEE PAGE 38)

1 In a large bowl, whisk together the flour, baking soda, cinnamon, nutmeg, cloves, and salt. Set aside.

2 In another large bowl, with an electric mixer, beat together the butter and sugar on medium speed until light, 2 to 3 minutes. Add the eggs, one at a time, beating well after each addition. Add the fruits and nuts and beat until evenly distributed. On low speed, gradually beat in the flour mixture just until mixed. The dough will be soft.

3 Gather the dough into a ball and wrap in plastic wrap. Refrigerate until firm, about 2 hours.

4 Preheat the oven to 375°F. Lightly grease or spray cookie sheets.

5 Drop the dough by slightly rounded tablespoons onto the cookie sheets, spacing them about 2 inches apart. Or, roll between your palms into balls about 1¼ inches in diameter.

LEMON ICING

3 CUPS CONFECTIONERS' SUGAR

3 TO 4 TABLESPOONS FRESH
LEMON JUICE

6 Bake in the center of the oven until just firm on top when lightly pressed with a fingertip and lightly golden on the bottom, about 8 minutes.

7 While the cookies are baking, prepare the icing. Sift the confectioners' sugar into a medium bowl. Whisk in enough lemon juice to make a smooth, spreadable icing. (Or, you can use a food processor to make the icing, omitting the sifting and processing until smooth and spreadable.)

8 When the cookies are ready, remove the cookie sheets from the oven. Using a pastry brush, brush the tops of the warm cookies with the icing. Transfer the cookies to wire racks to cool completely.

makes
34
cookies

LEMON-ICED COOKIES

You can enhance the flavor of these cookies by adding 1 tablespoon finely grated lemon zest to the icing. This dough can also be rolled out on a lightly floured board or pastry cloth and cut into shapes.

COOKIE EXCHANGE TIP: Many bakers strive to make their Christmas cookies festive, and you don't want yours to be lost in the crowd. With that in mind, we have added a sparkle to the icing—lemon-flavored jelly beans or yellow decorating sugar will work—on these citrusy cookies. Or, if you are pressed for time, you can leave the icing plain. The cookies will still be delicious.

3 CUPS ALL-PURPOSE FLOUR

½ TEASPOON BAKING SODA

½ TEASPOON SALT

½ CUP (1 STICK) UNSALTED BUTTER, AT ROOM TEMPERATURE

¾ CUP GRANULATED SUGAR

1 LARGE EGG

3 TABLESPOONS FRESH LEMON JUICE

LEMON ICING

3 CUPS CONFECTIONERS' SUGAR

3 TO 4 TABLESPOONS FRESH LEMON JUICE

ABOUT 68 LEMON-FLAVORED JELLY BEANS OR YELLOW DECORATING SUGAR FOR GARNISH

1 Preheat the oven to 375°F. Lightly grease or spray cookie sheets.

2 In a medium bowl, whisk together the flour, baking soda, and salt. Set aside.

3 In a large bowl, with an electric mixer, beat together the butter and granulated sugar on medium speed until light, about 2 minutes. Beat in the egg and lemon juice. On low speed, gradually beat in the flour mixture just until mixed. The dough should be smooth and slightly stiff.

4 Drop the dough by teaspoons onto the prepared cookie sheets, spacing them about 1⅛ inches apart. (Or, roll between your palms into 1-inch balls.) Lightly flatten each cookie with the bottom of a drinking glass.

5 Bake in the center of the oven until firm to the touch and golden brown on the bottom, about 10 minutes. Let cool on the cookie sheets for 2 minutes, then transfer to wire racks to cool completely.

6 Prepare the icing. Sift the confectioners' sugar into a medium bowl. Whisk in enough lemon juice to make a smooth, spreadable icing. (Or, you can use a food processor to make the icing, omitting the sifting and processing until smooth and spreadable.)

7 Using a pastry brush, brush the tops of the cooled cookies with the icing. Set 2 jelly beans on top of each cookie, or sprinkle the icing with the yellow sugar. Let the cookies stand on the wire racks until the icing sets.

SMALL
BLACK AND WHITES

makes
45
cookies

These classic cookies become more comfortable to handle when they are made mini size.

COOKIE EXCHANGE TIP: You can sprinkle a little red or green decorating sugar on the white frosting to add a festive twist to these already-handsome cookies. Store them in a single layer on 1 or more plates or trays, covered with waxed paper, until serving, then present them in a straw basket with a large red bow tied around the handle for a splash of color.

4 CUPS CAKE FLOUR

1½ TEASPOONS BAKING POWDER

¼ TEASPOON SALT

1½ CUPS VEGETABLE SHORTENING

1 CUP GRANULATED SUGAR

½ CUP NONFAT DRY MILK POWDER

1 TEASPOON LIGHT CORN SYRUP

3 LARGE EGGS

¾ CUP WATER

1¼ TEASPOONS VANILLA EXTRACT

ICING

2 CUPS CONFECTIONERS' SUGAR

1 TABLESPOON LIGHT CORN SYRUP

3 TO 4 TABLESPOONS WATER OR MILK, OR AS NEEDED

1 TEASPOON VANILLA EXTRACT

⅓ CUP UNSWEETENED COCOA POWDER

1   Preheat the oven to 350°F. Lightly grease or spray cookie sheets.

2   In a large bowl, whisk together the flour, baking powder, and salt. Set aside.

3   In a large bowl, with an electric mixer, beat together the shortening and granulated sugar on medium speed until light, 2 to 3 minutes. Beat in the dry milk powder and corn syrup. Add the eggs, one at a time, beating well after each addition. On low speed, gradually beat in the flour mixture, then the water and vanilla. The dough will be firm.

4   Pinch off pieces of dough and roll between your palms into 1¼-inch balls. Set on the prepared cookie sheets, spacing them about 2 inches apart.

5   Bake in the center of the oven until firm when lightly touched with a fingertip and a toothpick inserted in the center comes out clean, 14 to 16 minutes. Let cool on the cookie sheets for 2 to 3 minutes, then transfer to wire racks to cool completely.

continued...

. . . continued

6 Prepare the icing. Sift the confectioners' sugar into a medium bowl. Add the corn syrup, 2 tablespoons of the water, and the vanilla and beat with an electric mixer on medium speed until smooth and creamy, adding more water, 1 tablespoon at a time, as needed to make a smooth, spreadable icing. (Or, you can use a food processor to make the icing, omitting the sifting and processing until smooth and spreadable.)

7 Transfer half of the icing to another bowl and stir in the cocoa powder, adding more water, ½ teaspoon at a time, as needed to thin to the same consistency as the white icing. Cover both icings with plastic wrap until ready to use.

8 To ice the cookies, using an icing spatula, spread a thin layer of the white icing over half of the top of each cookie. Starting with the cookies you iced first (so the white icing has time to dry), spread the chocolate icing over the other half. Let the cookies stand until the icing dries.

GREEN TEA–
LEMON WAFERS

makes
40
cookies

Powdered green tea, or *matcha*, is available in some supermarkets and in Japanese markets and most other Asian markets.

COOKIE EXCHANGE TIP: Thanks to the addition of green tea, these wafers have a green tinge. A bit of red decorating sugar offsets the color nicely. Sprinkle it on the cookies after baking.

½ CUP (1 STICK) UNSALTED BUTTER

½ CUP GRANULATED SUGAR

1 TABLESPOON HONEY

1 EGG

1 TABLESPOON GREEN TEA POWDER

⅔ CUP SIFTED ALL-PURPOSE FLOUR

RED DECORATING SUGAR FOR SPRINKLING (OPTIONAL)

1 Preheat the oven to 350°F. Lightly grease or spray cookie sheets.

2 In a small saucepan, heat the butter, granulated sugar, and honey over medium heat, stirring occasionally, until the butter is melted. Remove from the heat. Whisk in the egg, then the green tea and flour to make a smooth batter.

3 Drop by teaspoons onto the prepared cookie sheets, spacing them about 2 inches apart.

4 Bake in the center of the oven until golden around the edges, 5 to 6 minutes. Let the wafers cool on the cookie sheets until they firm up, 3 to 4 minutes, then carefully transfer to wire racks.

5 Sprinkle the cookies with the decorating sugar, if using, while they are still warm, then let cool completely. They will be crisp when fully cooled.

makes about
48
cookies

CANDIED-FRUIT
FLORENTINES

These are a delight for the eyes as well as the palate. Candied fruit is embedded in a delicate wafer with a chocolate bottom. Change the bittersweet chocolate to white chocolate or semisweet chocolate, as you like.

COOKIE EXCHANGE TIP: These wafer cookies are delicate, so pack them carefully for transporting. Line the box with paper towels and use waxed paper or parchment paper between layers.

⅓ CUP (5½ TABLESPOONS) UNSALTED BUTTER

⅔ CUP SUGAR

½ CUP HEAVY CREAM

2 TABLESPOONS HONEY

⅓ CUP ALL-PURPOSE FLOUR

¼ CUP FINELY CHOPPED CANDIED LEMON PEEL

½ CUP CHOPPED RED CANDIED CHERRIES

1 CUP SLICED ALMONDS, PREFER-ABLY TOASTED (SEE PAGE 38)

6 OUNCES BITTERSWEET CHOCOLATE, CHOPPED

1 Preheat the oven to 350°F. Lightly grease or spray cookie sheets, then dust with flour and tap out the excess.

2 In a heavy, medium saucepan, combine the butter, sugar, cream, and honey. Place over medium heat and heat, stirring occasionally, until the butter melts and the mixture comes to a boil. Increase the heat to high and continue cooking for about 2 minutes, stirring often.

3 Remove from the heat and stir in the flour, lemon peel, cherries, and almonds. Let the batter stand for 10 minutes, stirring occasionally.

4 Drop the batter by rounded teaspoons onto the cookie sheets, spacing them 2½ to 3 inches apart. Try to keep the cookies round.

5 Bake in the center of the oven until the edges are golden brown, 10 to 12 minutes. The cookies will be thin and lacy. Let cool on the cookie sheets for 3 to 5 minutes, then use a spatula to transfer them carefully to a plate to cool completely.

6 Place the chocolate in a microwave-safe bowl or in the top of a double boiler. Microwave at 80 percent power or heat over (not touching) barely simmering water, stirring occasionally, until melted and smooth (see page 67).

7 Line cookie sheets with aluminum foil or parchment paper. Turn the cookies upside down on the lined sheets. Using a pastry brush or knife, spread the melted chocolate evenly over the bottoms of the cookies. Let stand on the cookie sheets at room temperature until the chocolate sets.

makes
40
cookies

MACAROONS WITH ALMOND PASTE

These are similar to the Amaretti on page 104, but they contain a bit of flour and are chewy on the inside, rather than crunchy all the way through.

COOKIE EXCHANGE TIP: Serve these aromatic cookies on a large plate garnished with sliced almonds.

1 (7- TO 8-OUNCE) CAN OR TUBE ALMOND PASTE

1 CUP GRANULATED SUGAR

3 LARGE EGG WHITES

¾ TEASPOON VANILLA EXTRACT

½ TEASPOON ALMOND EXTRACT

3 TABLESPOONS ALL-PURPOSE FLOUR

⅓ CUP CONFECTIONERS' SUGAR

¼ TEASPOON SALT

1 Break the almond paste into small pieces in a large bowl. With an electric mixer, beat in the granulated sugar and egg whites on medium speed until the mixture is well blended and soft. Beat in the vanilla and almond extracts, flour, confectioners' sugar, and salt until well mixed.

2 Line 2 cookie sheets with parchment paper. Drop the batter by teaspoons onto the prepared cookie sheets, spacing them about 1⅛ inches apart. Let the cookies stand at room temperature for 1⅛ hours to dry out. Do not let them stand longer than that.

3 Preheat the oven to 300°F.

4 Bake the cookies in the center of the oven until they are firm to the touch and have colored slightly, about 30 minutes. Just before they are ready, soak 2 kitchen towels in water and squeeze dry. Spread each towel out on a counter. When the cookies are done, carefully lift them, still on the parchment, onto the towels. (This will create steam to release the cookies.) Let stand for 5 to 10 minutes, or until you can easily remove the cookies from the parchment. Transfer the cookies to wire racks to cool completely.

KRIS KRINGLE COOKIES

makes
42
cookies

These treats, also known as crinkle-top cookies, are rolled in confectioners' sugar before, rather than after, baking, to produce an attractive dark cookie with a white crackled top.

COOKIE EXCHANGE TIP: Stuff old (clean!) mittens with tissue. Attach them, palm up, to a cardboard round and put the plate of cookies on top of the round. The plate will look like it is being served by mittened hands.

4 OUNCES UNSWEETENED BAKING CHOCOLATE, CHOPPED

4 TABLESPOONS (½ STICK) UNSALTED BUTTER, CUT INTO CHUNKS

2 CUPS ALL-PURPOSE FLOUR

2 CUPS GRANULATED SUGAR

4 LARGE EGGS

2 TEASPOONS BAKING POWDER

¼ TEASPOON GROUND CINNAMON

½ CUP CHOPPED HAZELNUTS OR WALNUTS, PREFERABLY TOASTED (SEE PAGE 38)

1¼ CUPS SIFTED CONFECTIONERS' SUGAR FOR ROLLING

1   Place the chocolate and butter in a microwave-safe bowl or in the top of a double boiler. Microwave at 80 percent power or heat over (not touching) barely simmering water, stirring occasionally, until melted and smooth (see page 67). Let cool.

2   In a large bowl, combine the cooled chocolate mixture, 1 cup of the flour, the granulated sugar, eggs, baking powder, and cinnamon. With an electric mixer, beat on medium speed until combined, about 2 minutes. Beat in the remaining 1 cup flour, then the nuts. The dough will be soft. Cover the bowl with plastic wrap or aluminum foil and refrigerate for at least 2 hours or up to 4 hours.

3   Preheat the oven to 350°F. Lightly grease or spray cookie sheets.

4   Spread the confectioners' sugar on a plate. Pinch off pieces of the dough and roll between your palms into 1¼-inch balls. Roll the balls in the sugar, coating them evenly. Place the coated balls on the prepared cookie sheets, spacing them about 2 inches apart.

5   Bake in the center of the oven until the tops are just firm when pressed lightly with a fingertip and the surface looks crackled, 12 to 15 minutes. Let cool on the cookie sheets for 2 minutes, then transfer to wire racks.

OATMEAL
BRICKLE NUGGETS

makes about 75 cookies

The toffee bits give the bottoms of these cookies a sugary-crunchy finish, making them truly irresistible.

COOKIE EXCHANGE TIP: These small cookies fit nicely in large, red and/or green plastic drinking cups. Place the cookies in the cups, then wrap each cup in plastic wrap or clear cellophane and tie with ribbon.

1 CUP (2 STICKS) UNSALTED BUTTER, AT ROOM TEMPERATURE

1 CUP FIRMLY PACKED LIGHT BROWN SUGAR

½ CUP GRANULATED SUGAR

1 LARGE EGG

1 TEASPOON VANILLA EXTRACT

1 TEASPOON BAKING POWDER

½ TEASPOON SALT

2 CUPS ALL-PURPOSE FLOUR

2 CUPS OLD-FASHIONED ROLLED OATS

1 (8-OUNCE) PACKAGE ENGLISH TOFFEE BITS (ABOUT 1⅓ CUPS)

1 Preheat the oven to 375°F. Lightly grease or spray cookie sheets.

2 In a large bowl, with an electric mixer, beat together the butter and brown and granulated sugars on medium speed until light, 2 to 3 minutes. Beat in the egg, vanilla, baking powder, and salt. On low speed, gradually beat in the flour just until mixed. Stir in the oats and toffee bits.

3 Pinch off pieces of the dough and roll between your palms into balls a bit larger than 1 inch in diameter. Place on the prepared cookie sheets, spacing them about 1¾ inches apart.

4 Bake in the center of the oven until firm to the touch and golden on the bottom and around the bottom edges, 10 to 12 minutes. Let cool on the cookie sheets for 1 minute, then transfer to wire racks to cool completely.

CHOCOLATE
MINCEMEAT JUMBLES

makes
48
cookies

Mincemeat, a mixture of raisins, dried apples, molasses, citrus peel, and a bit of beef suet, is available in some supermarkets year-round and in many supermarkets during the holiday season.

COOKIE EXCHANGE TIP: For a festive splash of color, top each cookie with half of a candied cherry.

2½ CUPS ALL-PURPOSE FLOUR

2 TEASPOONS BAKING SODA

½ TEASPOON SALT

½ CUP (1 STICK) UNSALTED BUTTER, AT ROOM TEMPERATURE

1 CUP SUGAR

3 LARGE EGGS

1 (12-OUNCE) PACKAGE SEMISWEET CHOCOLATE CHIPS (ABOUT 2 CUPS)

1 CUP PREPARED MINCEMEAT

1   Preheat the oven to 375°F. Lightly grease or spray cookie sheets.

2   In a medium bowl, whisk together the flour, baking soda, and salt. Set aside.

3   In a large bowl, with an electric mixer, beat together the butter and sugar on medium speed until light, 2 to 3 minutes. Add the eggs, one at a time, beating well after each addition. On low speed, gradually beat in the flour mixture just until mixed. Stir in the chocolate chips and mincemeat. The dough will be firm.

4   Drop by tablespoons onto the prepared cookie sheets, spacing them about 2⅛ inches apart.

5   Bake in the center of the oven until golden, 8 to 10 minutes. Let cool on the cookie sheets for 2 minutes, then transfer to wire racks to cool completely.

CHOCOLATE-
ORANGE COOKIES

makes about
48
cookies

For a particularly mellow flavor and dark color, use dark cocoa powder
(see page 66).

COOKIE EXCHANGE TIP: Decorate the cookie plate with chocolate-dipped
orange slices.

2 CUPS ALL-PURPOSE FLOUR

**½ CUP UNSWEETENED COCOA
POWDER, PREFERABLY DARK**

**2 TABLESPOONS FINELY GRATED
ORANGE ZEST**

**1¼ CUPS (2½ STICKS) UNSALTED
BUTTER, AT ROOM TEMPERATURE**

¾ CUP GRANULATED SUGAR

1 TEASPOON VANILLA EXTRACT

**1 CUP CHOPPED WALNUTS, HAZEL-
NUTS, OR ALMONDS, PREFERABLY
TOASTED (SEE PAGE 38)**

**ABOUT ½ CUP WHITE DECORATING
SUGAR OR GRANULATED SUGAR**

1 In a medium bowl, whisk together the flour, cocoa powder, and
   orange zest. Set aside.

2 In a large bowl, with an electric mixer, beat together the butter and
   granulated sugar on medium speed until light, 2 to 3 minutes. Beat in
   the vanilla. On low speed, beat in the flour mixture just until mixed.
   Stir in the nuts. The dough will still be soft, with the consistency of
   brownie batter.

3 Remove the batter from the bowl and wrap in plastic wrap. Refrigerate until firm enough to shape, 2 to 4 hours.

4 Preheat the oven to 350°F. Have ready ungreased cookie sheets.

5 Spread the decorating sugar on a plate. Pinch off pieces of the dough
   and roll between your palms into walnut-sized balls. Roll the balls in
   the sugar, coating evenly. Place on the cookie sheets, spacing them
   about 1½ inches apart.

6 Bake in the center of the oven until just firm to the touch when lightly
   pressed with a fingertip, 15 to 18 minutes. Let cool for 2 minutes on the
   cookie sheets, then transfer to wire racks to cool completely.

CHAPTER
2

BARS AND SQUARES

We like bar cookies for two reasons: many of them are easy to make and most of them fall into the gooey dessert category. Who can resist a chewy brownie or a buttery crust topped with a gooey filling?

If you are pressed for time, you can bake many drop cookie recipes (such as chocolate chip cookies) as bar cookies. Just spread the dough in a 9-by-13-inch or 10-by-15-inch pan and add 8 to 10 minutes to the baking time.

Most bar cookie recipes are relatively simple to make. They often include a crust and a filling that are easily layered in a pan for baking, and then the cooled layers are cut into neat rectangles or squares. Here is a handful of tips for making these baker's classics even more delicious and attractive:

1. For two-step bar cookies with a shortbread crust, bake the crust completely before adding the topping. When in doubt, slightly overbake the crust. Otherwise, it can absorb too much moisture from the filling and turn pasty.

2. Treat bars with custard fillings as you would custard pies. Let them cool, then keep them in the refrigerator and eat them within a day or two.

3. Do not underbake cake-style bars, or they will be gummy. Brownies are an exception; if you like them extra fudgy, underbake them slightly. (On the other hand, remember they *are* brownies, not fudge.) Be careful not to overbake, too, or the bars will be dry and crumbly.

4. Use a thin offset spatula or icing spatula to remove the cut bars from the pan.

5. Always allow the uncut bar to cool completely before cutting, unless a recipe instructs otherwise. If you cut it when it is still warm, it can crumble.

6. For the neatest bar cookies, line the baking pan with heavy-duty foil (or a double layer of regular foil), allowing it to extend slightly over two sides of the pan (on a rectangular pan, the two long sides). When the pan comes out of the oven and the whole bar has cooled, use these "handles" to lift the bar out of the pan for cutting. This makes it easy to trim off the uneven edges and to cut neat, even rectangles or squares. You may have to add 2 to 3 minutes to the baking time if using foil.

DATE-FILLED BARS

This is a classic bar cookie: a gooey date filling sandwiched between oat crusts. Our version is a tad less sweet than some.

COOKIE EXCHANGE TIP: Have some old 33 rpm records around the house? Cover them with decorative foil and use them as serving platters for the holidays. (Virginia got this tip from her Mom, Fran Van Vynckt, who always brings her upside-down pineapple cake to reunions on a foil-wrapped LP.) Because records don't have sides, they work best for serving bar cookies that won't slide.

FILLING

3 CUPS CHOPPED DATES (ABOUT 12 OUNCES)

1 CUP ORANGE JUICE

2 TABLESPOONS FIRMLY PACKED LIGHT BROWN SUGAR

1 TEASPOON VANILLA EXTRACT

CRUST AND TOPPING

2¾ CUPS OLD-FASHIONED ROLLED OATS

1 CUP ALL-PURPOSE FLOUR

¾ CUP FIRMLY PACKED LIGHT BROWN SUGAR

1 TEASPOON GROUND CINNAMON

½ TEASPOON SALT

1 CUP (2 STICKS) COLD UNSALTED BUTTER, CUT INTO TABLESPOON-SIZE CHUNKS

1 Prepare the filling. In a heavy saucepan, combine the dates, orange juice, brown sugar, and vanilla over medium heat. Cook, stirring occasionally, until the dates have cooked down to a thick paste, 5 to 7 minutes. Remove from the heat and let cool completely.

2 Preheat the oven to 350°F. Line a 9-by-13-inch baking pan with heavy-duty aluminum foil, letting it slightly overhang the long sides of the pan. (These "handles" will make it easier to lift the whole baked bar from the pan.)

3 Prepare the crust and topping. In a food processor, combine the oats, flour, brown sugar, cinnamon, and salt and pulse until thoroughly mixed. Scatter the butter pieces over the top and pulse just until a moist, crumbly dough forms. (Or, mix the dry ingredients in a large bowl and cut in the butter with 2 knives or a pastry blender until a moist, crumbly dough forms.)

4 Pat a little more than half of the oat dough evenly over the bottom of the pan. Spread the cooled filling over the crust. Top the filling with the remaining oat dough, and pat gently and evenly over the filling.

5 Bake in the center of the oven until the topping is golden around the edges, 30 to 35 minutes. Let cool completely in the pan on a wire rack. Then, using the foil, lift out of the pan and cut into bars.

RASPBERRY
LINZER SQUARES

makes **30** bars

Raspberry is the traditional filling for Linzer squares, but you can use apricot or another flavor jam if you prefer.

COOKIE EXCHANGE TIP: Linzer squares keep well, so you can make them 2 or 3 days before the exchange. Sprinkle with confectioners' sugar and sprinkle with the nuts just before leaving for the party.

½ CUP (1 STICK) UNSALTED BUTTER, AT ROOM TEMPERATURE

2 CUPS ALL-PURPOSE FLOUR

½ TEASPOON BAKING POWDER

1 CUP GROUND ALMONDS OR ALMOND MEAL

½ CUP GRANULATED SUGAR

2 TABLESPOONS UNSWEETENED COCOA POWDER

1 TEASPOON GROUND CINNAMON

¼ TEASPOON GROUND CLOVES

¼ TEASPOON SALT

FINELY GRATED ZEST OF 1 LEMON

3 LARGE EGG YOLKS

1 TEASPOON VANILLA EXTRACT

1 (12-OUNCE) JAR SEEDLESS RASPBERRY OR APRICOT JAM (ABOUT 1 CUP)

CONFECTIONERS' SUGAR FOR DUSTING

CHOPPED PISTACHIOS FOR SPRINKLING (OPTIONAL)

1   In a large bowl, with an electric mixer, beat together the butter, flour and baking powder on medium speed until blended, 1½ to 2 minutes. Add the almonds, granulated sugar, cocoa powder, cinnamon, cloves, salt, lemon zest, egg yolks, and vanilla and beat until a soft dough forms.

2   Gather the dough into a ball. Divide it into 2 portions, one about twice as large as the other, and wrap separately in plastic wrap. Refrigerate until firm, about 1 hour.

3   Preheat the oven to 350°F. Lightly grease or spray a nonstick 10-by-15-inch baking pan.

4   Place the larger dough portion in the prepared pan, and pat it evenly over the bottom and ½ inch up the sides. Using the back of a spoon, spread the jam evenly over the crust. Set aside.

5   Roll out the smaller dough portion on a lightly floured pastry cloth or board into a sheet 10 inches long and ⅛ inch thick. Cut the dough into strips 10 inches long and ⅜ inch wide. (Or, pinch off pieces of the dough and roll with your palms into ropes about ⅜ inch in diameter and 10 inches long.) Lay the dough strips over the jam-filled crust in a lattice design. You will need to piece together some of the strips to make them fit.

6   Bake in the center of the oven until the lattice crust is firm to the touch and lightly golden, about 20 minutes. Let cool in the pan on a wire rack. Using a sharp knife, cut into rectangles or squares, then carefully remove from the pan with a small offset spatula or an icing spatula.

7   Just before serving, sift the confectioners' sugar over the top, then sprinkle with the pistachios, if desired.

CROATIAN JAM-FILLED WALNUT

MERINGUE BARS

makes
35
bars

Variations of this bar cookie are popular in Croatia and throughout much of the rest of Europe: a sweet filling on a buttery crust, topped with jam and a crunchy walnut meringue.

COOKIE EXCHANGE TIP: Arrange these pretty bars in a rectangular straw bread basket lined with holiday-themed napkins.

CRUST

1 CUP (2 STICKS) UNSALTED BUTTER, AT ROOM TEMPERATURE

½ CUP SUGAR

½ TEASPOON GROUND CINNAMON

¼ TEASPOON SALT

1 LARGE EGG YOLK

2½ CUPS ALL-PURPOSE FLOUR

FILLING

¾ CUP SEEDLESS BLACKBERRY OR RASPBERRY JAM OR CURRANT JELLY

TOPPING

4 LARGE EGG WHITES, AT ROOM TEMPERATURE

2 TEASPOONS FRESH LEMON JUICE

1 CUP SUGAR

¾ CUP GROUND WALNUTS

½ CUP FINELY CHOPPED WALNUTS, PREFERABLY TOASTED (SEE PAGE 38)

1 Preheat the oven to 350°F. Lightly grease or spray a 10-by-15-inch baking pan.

2 Prepare the crust. In a large bowl, with an electric mixer, beat together the butter, sugar, cinnamon, and salt on medium speed until light, about 2 minutes. On low speed, beat in the egg yolk, then gradually beat in the flour just until mixed. The dough will be stiff and crumbly. Scrape it into the prepared pan and pat it evenly over the bottom. Using the back of a spoon, spread the jam evenly over the crust. Set aside.

3 Prepare the topping. In a large bowl, with the electric mixer, beat together the egg whites and lemon juice on high speed until foamy. On high speed, beat in the sugar, about 1 tablespoon at a time, and continue to beat until stiff, glossy peaks form, 2 to 3 minutes. Using a rubber spatula, fold in the ground nuts. Spoon the meringue over the jam and spread evenly. Sprinkle with the chopped nuts.

4 Bake in the center of the oven until the meringue is firm to the touch, 30 to 40 minutes. Let cool completely in the pan on a wire rack. Using a sharp knife, cut into bars, dipping the knife into hot water and wiping it dry before each cut. Carefully remove the bars from the pan with a small offset spatula or an icing spatula.

FIVE-LAYER BARS

makes
36
bars

To make cutting these sticky bars easier, be sure to heat the knife by dipping it into a glass of hot water and wiping it dry before each cut.

COOKIE EXCHANGE TIP: Supersweet and rich, these multilayered bars are an old favorite and can be made at nearly the last minute. When packing the bars for storage or transport, use waxed paper between the layers to keep them from sticking to one another.

½ CUP PLUS 2 TABLESPOONS (1¼ STICKS) UNSALTED BUTTER, CUT INTO CHUNKS

2 CUPS GRAHAM CRACKER CRUMBS

1 CUP SEMISWEET CHOCOLATE CHIPS

1 (14-OUNCE) CAN SWEETENED CONDENSED MILK

1½ CUPS SWEETENED SHREDDED OR FLAKED COCONUT

1 CUP CHOPPED PECANS

1 Preheat the oven to 350°F.

2 Place the chunks of butter in a 9-by-13-inch baking pan. Place the pan in the oven until the butter melts, 2 to 3 minutes.

3 Remove the pan from the oven and sprinkle the graham cracker crumbs evenly over the bottom of the pan. Press lightly to create an even layer.

4 Sprinkle the chocolate chips evenly over the crumb layer. Pour the condensed milk evenly over the chocolate chip layer. Sprinkle the coconut evenly over the milk layer, and then top evenly with the pecans.

5 Bake in the center of the oven until golden and bubbly, 20 to 25 minutes. Let cool completely in the pan on a wire rack. Using a small, sharp knife, cut into bars, dipping the knife into hot water and wiping it dry before each cut. Carefully remove the bars from the pan with a small offset spatula or an icing spatula.

APRICOT BARS

These bars are particularly rich and sweet, so we cut them smaller than many other bar cookies.

COOKIE EXCHANGE TIP: Just before serving or packaging, dust these bars with a very light coating of confectioners' sugar.

CRUST

¾ CUP (1½ STICKS) COLD UNSALTED BUTTER, CUT INTO CHUNKS

1¾ CUPS ALL-PURPOSE FLOUR

¾ CUP GRANULATED SUGAR

FILLING

¾ CUP DRIED APRICOTS, CHOPPED

¾ CUP WATER

1 CUP APRICOT PRESERVES

¼ CUP FIRMLY PACKED DARK BROWN SUGAR

4 LARGE EGGS

¼ TEASPOON SALT

1 TEASPOON VANILLA EXTRACT

1 Preheat the oven to 350°F. Lightly grease or spray a 9-inch square baking pan or line it with baking parchment.

2 Prepare the crust. In a food processor, combine the butter, flour, and sugar and pulse for a few seconds until a crumbly dough forms. Remove half of the mixture from the processor and set aside to use for the topping. Pat the remaining half of the mixture evenly over the bottom of the prepared baking pan.

3 Bake in the center of the oven until lightly golden, about 20 minutes.

4 While the crust is baking, prepare the filling. In a heavy, medium saucepan, combine the dried apricots and water over medium heat. Cook until all of the water is absorbed and the apricots are soft, about 8 minutes. Remove from the heat and let cool for 5 minutes.

5 Transfer the apricots to the food processor and process to a smooth paste. Add the apricot preserves, brown sugar, eggs, salt, and vanilla and process until thoroughly combined.

continued . . .

... *continued*

6 Remove the crust from the oven. Using a rubber spatula or an icing spatula, carefully spread the filling evenly over the hot crust. Then sprinkle the reserved crust mixture evenly over the filling.

7 Return the pan to the oven and bake until the top is golden brown, 35 to 45 minutes. Let cool completely in the pan on a wire rack. Using a sharp knife, cut into bars, dipping the knife into hot water and wiping it dry before each cut. Carefully remove the bars from the pan with a small offset spatula or an icing spatula.

OLD-FASHIONED
APPLE SQUARES

Use a tart apple, such as Granny Smith or Jonathan, to make these cakelike bars.

COOKIE EXCHANGE TIP: To give these traditional treats rustic holiday flair, weave raffia around the edges of a wicker liner, then place the squares on a paper plate in the liner.

2 CUPS ALL-PURPOSE FLOUR

2 TEASPOONS BAKING SODA

¼ TEASPOON SALT

1¼ TEASPOONS GROUND CINNAMON

¼ TEASPOON GROUND NUTMEG

¼ TEASPOON GROUND GINGER

½ CUP (1 STICK) UNSALTED BUTTER, AT ROOM TEMPERATURE

2 CUPS GRANULATED SUGAR

2 LARGE EGGS

4 CUPS FINELY DICED UNPEELED APPLES

½ CUP CHOPPED PECANS OR WALNUTS, PREFERABLY TOASTED (SEE PAGE 38)

½ CUP DARK RAISINS

CONFECTIONERS' SUGAR FOR DUSTING

1 Preheat the oven to 325°F. Lightly grease or spray a 9-by-13-inch baking pan.

2 In a medium bowl, whisk together the flour, baking soda, salt, cinnamon, nutmeg, and ginger. Set aside.

3 In a large bowl, with an electric mixer, beat together the butter and granulated sugar on medium speed until light, 2 to 3 minutes. Beat in the eggs. On low speed, gradually beat in the flour mixture just until mixed. The batter will be thick. Stir in the apples, nuts, and raisins, distributing them evenly. Spoon the batter into the prepared pan, spreading it evenly.

4 Bake in the center of the oven until golden on top, 45 to 50 minutes. Let cool completely in the pan on a wire rack. Using a sharp knife, cut into 2-inch squares, then carefully remove from the pan with a small offset spatula or an icing spatula. Sift the confectioners' sugar over the tops.

makes
35
bars

LEMON BARS WITH A COCONUT CRUST

Toasted coconut gives a boost to the traditional lemon bar. This bar cookie has a thin, crunchy crust. For a thicker crust, make the recipe in a 9-by-13-inch baking pan and use only 4 eggs and ½ cup lemon juice in the topping.

COOKIE EXCHANGE TIP: These are sticky, so use waxed paper between the layers when you pack them for transport or storage. Keep them in the refrigerator until it is time to carry them to the cookie exchange, and then set them out on a doily-lined plate.

CRUST

1 CUP (2 STICKS) UNSALTED BUTTER, AT ROOM TEMPERATURE

½ CUP CONFECTIONERS' SUGAR

2 CUPS ALL-PURPOSE FLOUR

½ CUP SWEETENED FLAKED COCONUT, TOASTED (SEE PAGE 38)

TOPPING

5 LARGE EGGS

2 CUPS GRANULATED SUGAR

⅔ CUP FRESH LEMON JUICE

FINELY GRATED ZEST OF 1 LEMON

1 TEASPOON BAKING POWDER

⅓ CUP SWEETENED FLAKED COCONUT, TOASTED

CONFECTIONERS' SUGAR FOR DUSTING

1 Preheat the oven to 350°F. Lightly grease or spray a 10-by-15-inch baking pan.

2 Prepare the crust. In a large bowl, with an electric mixer, beat together the butter and confectioners' sugar on medium speed until light, 2 to 3 minutes. On low speed, gradually beat in the flour, then the coconut until a stiff, crumbly dough forms. Transfer the dough to the prepared pan and press it evenly over the bottom.

3 Bake in the center of the oven until lightly golden, about 10 minutes.

4 While the crust is baking, prepare the topping. In a large bowl, with the electric mixer, beat together the eggs and granulated sugar on high speed until thick and light, about 3 minutes. Beat in the lemon juice, lemon zest, and baking powder just until mixed.

5 Remove the crust from the oven. Pour the topping evenly over the hot crust.

6 Return the pan to the oven and bake until the topping is set and beginning to brown lightly, about 10 minutes. Remove from the oven and sprinkle evenly with the coconut. Press the coconut lightly into the lemon topping. Let cool completely in the pan on a wire rack.

7 Sift the confectioners' sugar evenly over the top, dusting lightly. Then, using a sharp knife, cut into bars. Carefully remove the bars from the pan with a small offset spatula or an icing spatula.

ITALIAN
TRICOLOR COOKIES

makes
36
cookies

Also called rainbow cookies, these striped treats have a texture more like petits fours than traditional cookies. If you don't have three 8-inch square baking pans, you can bake the layers one at a time. Or, use 8-inch square disposable foil pans.

COOKIE EXCHANGE TIP: These cookies should resemble the Italian flag, so be sure to follow the recipe closely and arrange the layers in the proper order.

1 (7- TO 8-OUNCE) CAN OR TUBE ALMOND PASTE

1 CUP (2 STICKS) UNSALTED BUTTER, AT ROOM TEMPERATURE, PLUS 2 TEASPOONS FOR CHOCOLATE TOPPING

¾ CUP SUGAR

3 LARGE EGGS

¼ TEASPOON ALMOND EXTRACT

½ TEASPOON SALT

1¼ CUPS ALL-PURPOSE FLOUR

RED GEL FOOD COLORING

GREEN GEL FOOD COLORING

¾ CUP APRICOT JAM

6 OUNCES BITTERSWEET CHOCOLATE, CHOPPED

1   Preheat the oven to 350°F. Lightly grease or spray three 8-inch square pans and line the bottoms with waxed paper. Grease or spray the waxed paper.

2   Break the almond paste into small pieces in a large bowl and add the butter and sugar. With an electric mixer, beat on medium speed just until mixed, about 1 minute. The mixture will be a bit lumpy. Add the eggs, almond extract, and salt and beat until light and smooth, about 1 minute. On low speed, gradually beat in the flour just until mixed. You will have a thick batter.

3   Transfer one-third of the batter (about 1 rounded cup) to a small bowl. Transfer another one-third to another small bowl. Leave the remaining one-third in the large bowl. Add 10 to 12 drops of red food coloring to 1 batch of the batter and mix well. Add 10 to 12 drops of green coloring to another batch of the batter and mix well. The red and green doughs should be deeply colored. Leave the remaining batter uncolored.

4   Scrape each batch of dough into one of the prepared pans. Use a wet rubber spatula or an icing spatula to smooth the top. The batter is thick and you may have to hold the edges of the waxed paper in place with your fingers to keep it from sliding.

5   Place the pans in the center of the oven on 2 oven racks, or place them on 1 rack on the diagonal if they will fit that way. Bake until a toothpick inserted in the center of a layer comes out clean, 10 to 12 minutes, switching the positions of the pans and rotating them front to back halfway through the baking time to ensure even baking. Let cool in the pans on wire racks for 20 minutes, then invert the layers onto the racks to cool completely.

6   Lay a piece of aluminum foil or waxed paper on the work surface. Place the green layer, waxed paper side up, on the foil, and peel off the waxed paper. Spread with half of the jam. Set the plain (uncolored) layer, waxed paper side up, on top, press gently, and then peel off the waxed paper. Spread with the remaining jam. Set the red layer, waxed paper side up, on top, press gently, and then peel off the waxed paper.

7   With a large, sharp knife, trim the sides of the cookie layers to make them even.

8   Place the chocolate and butter in a microwave-safe bowl or in the top of a double boiler. Microwave at 80 percent power or heat over (not touching) barely simmering water, stirring occasionally, until melted and smooth (see page 67). Let the chocolate cool until it is thick enough to spread over the top of the cookie layers without dripping down the sides.

9   Spread the chocolate evenly over the top of the red layer (do not spread the chocolate on the sides). If desired, run the tines of a fork through the melted chocolate to make a wavy design.

10 Let stand until the chocolate sets, about 30 minutes. (Or, refrigerate to set the chocolate more quickly.) Cut the stacked layers into 6 equal strips. Then cut 6 equal strips perpendicular to the first strips, to make square cookies.

GREEK
CUSTARD BARS

makes
36
bars

Phyllo, paper-thin pastry that crisps up as it bakes, is available at Greek and Middle Eastern markets and in many supermarkets. It is usually in the freezer case. Look for semolina flour, finely ground durum wheat often labeled "pasta flour," in Italian, Greek, Middle Eastern, and Indian groceries; health food stores; and well-stocked supermarkets.

COOKIE EXCHANGE TIP: Arrange these luscious custard squares, known as *bougatsa* in Greece, in a single layer on a platter decorated with several Christmas ornaments.

FILLING

½ CUP (1 STICK) UNSALTED BUTTER

¾ CUP SEMOLINA FLOUR

4 CUPS MILK, SCALDED AND COOLED

¾ CUP SUGAR

2 LARGE EGGS, LIGHTLY BEATEN

2 LARGE EGG YOLKS, LIGHTLY BEATEN

1¼ TEASPOONS VANILLA EXTRACT

18 SHEETS PHYLLO DOUGH (ABOUT 8 OUNCES), THAWED ACCORDING TO PACKAGE DIRECTIONS

½ CUP (1 STICK) UNSALTED BUTTER, MELTED AND COOLED

1   Prepare the filling. In a heavy saucepan, melt the butter over medium heat. Stir in the semolina. Continue stirring as you gradually add the milk and sugar. Reduce the heat to medium-low and continue cooking, stirring often, until the mixture thickens enough to coat a spoon, about 10 minutes.

2   Remove from the heat and cover with plastic wrap, pressing it directly onto the surface to prevent a skin from forming. Let cool completely. The cooled filling should be thick but pourable. Stir in the eggs, egg yolks, and vanilla, mixing well. Set aside.

3   Preheat the oven to 375°F. Lightly grease or spray a 9-by-13-inch baking pan.

4   Remove the phyllo sheets from their package, unroll them, and keep them covered with plastic wrap and a dampened kitchen towel to prevent the sheets you are not immediately working with from drying out. Lay 1 sheet in the bottom of the prepared pan (it will reach up the sides), and brush lightly with the melted butter. Top with a second sheet and again brush lightly with the butter. Repeat until you have stacked a total of 12 phyllo sheets, brushing each one lightly with the butter.

5 Pour the cooled custard evenly over the phyllo, and fold the edges of the phyllo sheets extending up the sides of the pan over the filling. Cover the custard with the remaining 6 phyllo sheets, again brushing each sheet lightly with butter as you stack it. Tuck under or trim excess phyllo dough. Brush the top with butter.

6 Bake in the center of the oven until golden brown, about 25 minutes. Let cool completely in the pan on a wire rack. The custard will firm up as it cools. Using a sharp knife, cut into pieces about 1 by 3 inches. Carefully remove the bars from the pan with a small offset spatula or an icing spatula.

CHOCOLATE-TOPPED

PECAN BARS

These rich bars are similar in flavor and texture to pecan pie.

COOKIE EXCHANGE TIP: If you have a 2- or 3-tiered server, use it to display these—and just about any other cookie—to advantage.

BASIC BUTTER COOKIES DOUGH (PAGE 150)

3 LARGE EGGS

¾ CUP FIRMLY PACKED LIGHT BROWN SUGAR

¼ CUP LIGHT CORN SYRUP

1 TEASPOON VANILLA EXTRACT

2 CUPS CHOPPED PECANS, PREFERABLY TOASTED (SEE PAGE 38)

1½ CUPS SEMISWEET CHOCOLATE CHIPS, BITTERSWEET CHOCOLATE CHIPS, OR CHOPPED BITTERSWEET CHOCOLATE

1 Make the butter cookies dough and refrigerate as directed.

2 Preheat the oven to 350°F. Lightly grease or spray a 9-by-13-inch baking pan, or line with foil.

3 Press the chilled dough evenly over the bottom of the prepared baking pan. Bake in the center of the oven just until golden, about 15 minutes.

4 While the crust is baking, in a large bowl, with an electric mixer, beat together the eggs, brown sugar, corn syrup, and vanilla until smooth. Stir in the nuts.

5 Remove the pan from the oven. Pour the egg mixture over the hot crust, then pick up the pan with pot holders and rock it gently back and forth to distribute the filling evenly.

6 Return the pan to the oven and bake until the topping is set and golden, 20 to 25 minutes.

7 Remove the pan from the oven and sprinkle the chocolate chips evenly over the top. Return the pan to the oven for 1 minute. Remove the pan again and, using a knife, spread the chocolate evenly over the crust.

8 Let cool completely in the pan on a wire rack. Using a sharp knife, cut into bars, then carefully remove from the pan with a small offset spatula or an icing spatula.

CEREAL BARS WITH
CHOCOLATE ON TOP

makes **32** bars

We have given these classic treats a new twist by mixing peanut butter with the cereal mixture and adding a chocolate topping.

COOKIE EXCHANGE TIP: Save your Christmas decorations from one year to the next, packed carefully and stored in a dry, cool area, then use them to dress up your cookie trays. For example, we know someone who stands a 6-inch decorated Christmas tree at the head of the cookie tray.

3 TABLESPOONS UNSALTED BUTTER OR MARGARINE

1 (10-OUNCE) PACKAGE REGULAR MARSHMALLOWS (ABOUT 40), OR 4 CUPS MINIATURE MARSHMALLOWS

½ CUP SMOOTH PEANUT BUTTER

6 CUPS CRISP TOASTED RICE CEREAL

12 OUNCES SEMISWEET OR MILK CHOCOLATE, CHOPPED

1 Butter a 9-by-13-inch baking pan.

2 In a large, heavy saucepan, melt the butter over low heat. Add the marshmallows and stir until completely melted. Remove from the heat. Stir in the peanut butter, then the rice cereal until evenly coated.

3 Transfer the cereal mixture to the prepared pan. Using the back of a spoon, press it evenly over the bottom. Let stand until firm and completely cool, about 15 minutes.

4 Meanwhile, place the chocolate in a microwave-safe bowl or in the top of a double boiler. Microwave at 80 percent power if using semisweet chocolate or 50 percent power if using milk chocolate, or heat over (not touching) barely simmering water. Stir occasionally until melted and smooth (see page 67).

5 Drizzle the chocolate evenly over the top. Let stand until the chocolate is set. Using a small, sharp knife, cut into bars, then carefully remove from the pan with a small offset spatula or an icing spatula.

TOFFEE SQUARES

makes
48
squares

To heighten the toffee flavor, substitute toffee baking bits for half of the chopped almonds.

COOKIE EXCHANGE TIP: This is another of those always-popular cookie-exchange selections: Toffee-laced squares appeal to just about everyone. Dress them up a little by weaving lengths of gold metallic ribbon through the stacked cookies.

CRUST

1 CUP (2 STICKS) UNSALTED BUTTER, AT ROOM TEMPERATURE

1 CUP FIRMLY PACKED LIGHT BROWN SUGAR

1 LARGE EGG YOLK

1 TEASPOON VANILLA EXTRACT

¼ TEASPOON SALT

2 CUPS ALL-PURPOSE FLOUR

TOPPING

7 TO 8 OUNCES MILK CHOCOLATE, BROKEN INTO PIECES, OR 1½ CUPS MILK CHOCOLATE CHIPS

1 CUP CHOPPED ALMONDS, TOASTED (SEE PAGE 38)

1   Preheat the oven to 350°F. Line a 9-by-13-inch baking pan with parchment.

2   Prepare the crust. In a large bowl, with an electric mixer, beat together the butter and sugar on medium speed until light, about 2 minutes. Beat in the egg yolk, vanilla, and salt. On low speed, gradually beat in the flour just until mixed. The dough will be stiff. Pat the dough evenly over the bottom of the baking pan.

3   Bake in the center of the oven until pale gold on top, about 20 minutes.

4   Remove the pan from the oven and scatter the chocolate pieces evenly over the crust. Return the pan to the oven for 1 minute. Remove the pan again and, using a knife, spread the chocolate evenly over the crust. Sprinkle evenly with the almonds.

5   Let cool completely in the pan on a wire rack. Using a sharp knife, cut into small squares, then carefully remove from the pan with a small offset spatula or an icing spatula.

CHAPTER
3

ROLLED AND CUTOUT COOKIES

What would Christmas be without cookies cut out in interesting shapes? Nowadays, cookie cutters come in an amazing array of shapes, from dinosaurs to skyscrapers to reindeer. To make your cookies even more eye-catching, buy a set of gum paste or mini cookie cutters that range in size from ½ inch to ¾ inch across, and cut out one or more shapes within each cookie.

Rolled cookies can pose some challenges, so here are a few "rules" to ensure success:

1. If the chilled dough is too hard to roll, let it stand at room temperature for 10 to 15 minutes to soften slightly. Before rolling, pat it firmly all over with the rolling pin to help make it more pliable.

2. If the dough starts to soften and become sticky as you are rolling, put it in the freezer for 5 to 10 minutes to firm it up.

3. Use as little flour as possible when rolling out the dough. Too much flour can result in a tough, pasty cookie. Fabric retains flour better than a smooth surface, so placing a pastry cloth on the board and a cloth sleeve on the rolling pin helps cut down on the amount of flour needed.

4. Roll out the dough to as even a thickness as possible. If some cookies are thinner than others, your batch will not come out evenly baked.

5. Tin (or other metal) cutters produce sharper outlines than plastic ones. Dip the cutting edge of the cutter lightly in flour to prevent sticking.

6. Cut straight up and down with a cutter in a single, quick motion. If you twist the cutter, you will blur the outlines of the cookie, or in the case of a leavened cookie, pinch the edges so it might not rise as much as it should.

7. Cut the cookies as close together as possible. The fewer scraps, the better. The scraps can be rerolled and cut again, but the cookies from the rerolled scraps will not be as tender. Generally, you can reroll the scraps twice without sacrificing too much quality.

BASIC
BUTTER COOKIES

makes **50** cookies

Butter cookies, as the name implies, have a high percentage of butter, making them tender, crisp, and not as sweet as sugar cookies. Here's a basic butter dough, which can be baked as is, made into a crust for Chocolate-Topped Pecan Bars (page 144), or rolled and cut to make Christmas Cutout Cookies (page 152).

COOKIE EXCHANGE TIP: To give cookies extra shine, sprinkle them with edible glitter, available at crafts stores and cake-decorating stores.

1 CUP (2 STICKS) UNSALTED BUTTER, AT ROOM TEMPERATURE

1 CUP GRANULATED SUGAR

1 LARGE EGG YOLK

1 TEASPOON VANILLA EXTRACT

¼ TEASPOON SALT

2 CUPS ALL-PURPOSE FLOUR

DECORATING SUGAR OR GRANULATED SUGAR FOR SPRINKLING

1   In a large bowl, with an electric mixer, beat together the butter and granulated sugar on medium speed until light, 2 to 3 minutes. Beat in the egg yolk, then the vanilla and salt. On low speed, gradually beat in the flour just until mixed. The dough should be medium-stiff.

2   Gather the dough into a ball, pat into a thick disk, and wrap in plastic wrap. Refrigerate until firm, at least 1 hour or up to 1 day.

3   Preheat the oven to 350°F. Lightly grease or spray cookie sheets.

4   Place the dough on a lightly floured pastry cloth or board, and roll out ¼ inch thick. Using a 2½-inch round cookie cutter, cut out cookies. Using a spatula, transfer the cookies to the prepared cookie sheets, spacing them about 1½ inches apart. Gather the scraps, reroll, and cut out more cookies. Sprinkle the cookies lightly with the decorating sugar.

5   Bake in the center of the oven until faintly golden, 8 to 10 minutes. Let cool on the cookie sheets for 1 minute, then transfer to wire racks to cool completely.

SANTA GRAHAMS

makes about 32 cookies

Homemade graham crackers cut into Santa shapes are cute, but you can also cut them into other seasonal shapes or into rounds, strips, or even the traditional squares.

COOKIE EXCHANGE TIP: Homemade graham crackers taste good plain, but you may want to dress them up for a cookie exchange. Cut them into fun shapes and sprinkle with cinnamon sugar before baking, or top with fondant icing (page 15) after baking. Better yet, use them as the base for Father Christmas S'mores (page 46).

1¼ CUPS ALL-PURPOSE FLOUR

1 CUP WHOLE-WHEAT FLOUR

½ TEASPOON BAKING POWDER

¾ TEASPOON GROUND CINNAMON

⅛ TEASPOON GROUND NUTMEG

¼ TEASPOON SALT

¾ CUP (1½ STICKS) UNSALTED BUTTER, AT ROOM TEMPERATURE

⅓ CUP FIRMLY PACKED LIGHT BROWN SUGAR

3 TABLESPOONS GRANULATED SUGAR

2 TABLESPOONS HONEY

1 LARGE EGG

1 TEASPOON VANILLA EXTRACT

1 In a medium bowl, whisk together the all-purpose and whole-wheat flours, baking powder, cinnamon, nutmeg, and salt. Set aside.

2 In a large bowl, with an electric mixer, beat together the butter and the brown and granulated sugars on medium speed until smooth and creamy, about 2 minutes. Beat in the honey, egg, and vanilla. On low speed, gradually beat in the flour mixture until a soft dough forms.

3 Divide the dough in half. Pat each half into a thick disk and wrap separately in plastic wrap. Refrigerate until firm, at least 2 hours or up to 1 day.

4 Preheat the oven to 350°F. Have ready nonstick cookie sheets. (Or, line regular cookie sheets with aluminum foil or parchment paper.)

5 Place 1 dough disk on a lightly floured pastry cloth or board, and roll out ⅛ inch to ¼ inch thick. Using a 3- to 3½-inch Santa cookie cutter, cut out cookies. Using a spatula, transfer the cookies to the cookie sheets, spacing them about 1½ inches apart. Repeat with the second dough disk. Combine the scraps, reroll, and cut out more cookies.

6 Bake in the center of the oven until just firm to the touch, about 8 minutes. Let cool on the cookie sheets for 2 minutes, then transfer to wire racks to cool completely.

CHRISTMAS
CUTOUT COOKIES

makes about 30 cookies

It is fun to vary the shape of these cookies with a wide variety of cookie cutters: Santas, snowmen, stockings, bells, angels, holly sprigs, gingerbread men and women, stars, candy canes, and assorted animals. Decorations can be simple or complicated and completely creative. Let the children help and make it a family project.

COOKIE EXCHANGE TIP: If you are in a hurry, skip the icing and sprinkle the cookies with decorating sugar or sprinkles before baking.

BASIC BUTTER COOKIES DOUGH (PAGE 150)

EASY VANILLA ICING (PAGE 16) OR POURED FONDANT ICING (PAGE 15)

FOOD COLORING IN COLOR(S) OF CHOICE (OPTIONAL)

DECORATING SUGAR, NONPAREILS, SPRINKLES, DECORATOR ICING, AND/ OR OTHER DECORATIONS AS DESIRED

1 Make the butter cookies dough and refrigerate as directed.

2 Preheat the oven to 350°F. Lightly grease or spray cookie sheets.

3 Place the dough on a lightly floured pastry cloth or board, and roll out ¼ inch thick. Cut out cookies with your favorite cookie cutters. Using a spatula, transfer the cookies to the prepared cookie sheets, spacing them about 1⅛ inches apart. Gather the scraps, reroll, and cut out more cookies.

4 Bake in the center of the oven until faintly golden, 8 to 10 minutes. Let cool on the cookie sheets for 1 minute, then transfer to wire racks to cool completely.

5 Make the icing as directed and leave it white or tint it with food coloring. Using an icing spatula or a spoon, cover the tops of the cookies with the icing. While the icing is still slightly moist (but not wet), sprinkle with the decorating sugar or other decorations. For example, we made holly cutouts, spread them with white icing, and then sprinkled the icing with green nonpareils and added dots of red decorator icing at the tip to look like berries. Or, let the icing dry to a smooth finish, then decorate with decorating pens, decorator icing, or food coloring painted on with a small brush.

CREAM CHEESE
SUGAR COOKIES WITH
DULCE DE LECHE

Dulce de leche, or milk caramel, has become a popular ingredient in baked goods. Even the Girl Scouts now offer a *dulce de leche* cookie. We love its gooey rich sweetness as a topping for sugar cookies.

COOKIE EXCHANGE TIP: Drizzle red and/or green decorator gel icing over a large white plate to give these cookies a restaurant-style presentation.

3¼ CUPS ALL-PURPOSE FLOUR

¾ TEASPOON BAKING POWDER

¼ TEASPOON SALT

1 CUP (2 STICKS) UNSALTED BUTTER, AT ROOM TEMPERATURE

1 (8-OUNCE) PACKAGE CREAM CHEESE, AT ROOM TEMPERATURE

2 CUPS SUGAR

1 LARGE EGG

2 TEASPOONS VANILLA EXTRACT

***DULCE DE LECHE* (RECIPE FOLLOWS)**

1 In a medium bowl, whisk together the flour, baking powder, and salt. Set aside.

2 In a large bowl, with an electric mixer, beat together the butter and cream cheese on medium speed until well blended. Add the sugar and beat until light, about 2 minutes. Beat in the egg and vanilla. On low speed, beat in the flour mixture just until mixed. The dough will be soft and sticky.

3 Divide the dough in half. Pat each half into a thick disk and wrap separately in plastic wrap. Refrigerate until firm, at least 2 hours or up to overnight.

4 Preheat the oven to 350°F. Lightly grease or spray cookie sheets.

5 Place 1 dough disk on a lightly floured pastry cloth or board, and roll out ¼ inch thick. Using a 2½-inch round cookie cutter, cut out cookies. Using a spatula, transfer the cookies to the prepared cookie sheets, spacing them about 2 inches apart. Repeat with the second dough disk. Combine the scraps, reroll, and cut out more cookies.

6 Bake in the center of the oven until firm to the touch and beginning to turn golden on the edges, 12 to 14 minutes. Let cool on the cookie sheets for 2 minutes, then transfer to wire racks to cool completely.

7 Put the *dulce de leche* into a microwave-safe bowl and heat in the microwave on 10 to 20 percent power (low) until pourable, 20 to 30 seconds. Or, put it in the top of a double boiler over (not touching) gently boiling water until pourable. Dip the tines of a fork in the caramel and drizzle decoratively over the cookies. Or, pour the warm caramel into a squeeze bottle and squeeze it over the cookies. Let stand until set, about 30 minutes.

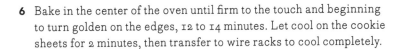

makes
3/4
cup

DULCE DE LECHE

Dulce de leche, roughly "milk candy," is caramelized milk and sugar. It is found under different names in several cultures: *cajeta* in Mexico, *confiture le lait* in France, *manjar blanco* in Peru. You can find ready-made *dulce de leche* or *cajeta* in some grocery stores, but it is easy to make yourself.

continued . . .

... *continued*

Many old recipes call for heating an unopened can of sweetened condensed milk in water to cover on the stovetop for several hours. We do *not* recommend this technique, however, because if the water level drops below the top of the can (which may well happen if you aren't paying close attention), the can could explode, causing a big mess in the kitchen or possibly an injury to you. The quickest way to make this caramel is in the microwave, though the timing can be tricky. The easiest, hands-off way to make it is in the oven. Here are both methods:

OVEN: Preheat the oven to 425°F. Place a 9-inch pie pan, preferably glass, in a shallow baking pan. Pour 1 (14-ounce) can sweetened condensed milk into the pie pan, and cover the pie pan with aluminum foil. Pour hot water into the baking pan to reach halfway up the sides of the pie pan. Bake until the milk is thick and a light caramel color, checking it after 40 minutes. It usually takes 50 to 60 minutes. Pour the hot caramel into a bowl and whisk or beat until smooth. It should be the consistency of a thick buttercream or pudding.

MICROWAVE: Pour 1 (14-ounce) can sweetened condensed milk into a 2- to 3-quart heatproof glass measuring pitcher or microwave-safe bowl. Microwave on 20 percent power (low) for 7 to 12 minutes, stirring frequently. The timing will vary according to the size and wattage of your microwave oven. As the milk cooks, it will boil and bubble up. When it begins to thicken, it will stop bubbling, and that is when you must start watching it carefully. It is ready when it is thick and a light caramel color. Whisk or beat until smooth. It should be the consistency of a thick buttercream or pudding.

Let the caramel cool, then cover tightly and refrigerate. It will keep for up to 1 week. When you are ready to use it, warm it for 20 to 30 seconds in a microwave oven on 10 to 20 percent power (low) or in the top of a double boiler over (not touching) gently boiling water until it is thin enough to be spooned or poured.

GERMAN
STREUSEL COOKIES

makes
42
cookies

If you have extra streusel, spoon it into a self-sealing plastic bag and freeze it for up to 3 months, then use it to top cookies or muffins.

COOKIE EXCHANGE TIP: For an elegant presentation, arrange these cookies on a silver tray lined with a doily.

2 CUPS ALL-PURPOSE FLOUR, SIFTED

1 TEASPOON BAKING POWDER

¾ CUP PLUS 2 TABLESPOONS (1¾ STICKS) UNSALTED BUTTER, AT ROOM TEMPERATURE

½ CUP SUGAR

1 LARGE EGG

1 TEASPOON VANILLA EXTRACT

¾ CUP GROUND ALMONDS

STREUSEL TOPPING

1½ CUPS ALL-PURPOSE FLOUR

¾ CUP SUGAR

½ TEASPOON GROUND CINNAMON

½ CUP (1 STICK) COLD UNSALTED BUTTER, CUT INTO SMALL PIECES

1 TEASPOON VANILLA EXTRACT

ABOUT 21 RED CANDIED CHERRIES OR DRAINED RED MARASCHINO CHERRIES, CUT IN HALF

1 In a large bowl, whisk together the flour and baking powder. Set aside.

2 In a large bowl, with an electric mixer, beat together the butter and sugar on medium speed until light, about 2 minutes. Beat in the egg, then the vanilla and almonds. On low speed, gradually beat in the flour mixture just until mixed. The dough will be stiff.

3 Gather the dough into a ball, then knead a few times in the bowl if necessary to make it smooth. Pat into a thick disk, wrap in plastic wrap, and refrigerate until firm, about 1 hour or up to overnight.

4 While the dough is chilling, prepare the topping. In a food processor, combine the flour, sugar, and cinnamon and pulse briefly to mix. Scatter the butter over the top, add the vanilla, and pulse just until the mixture is moist and crumbly. (Or, whisk the dry ingredients together in a medium bowl, add the butter and vanilla, and beat with an electric mixer on low speed just until the mixture is moist and crumbly.)

5   Preheat the oven to 375°F. Lightly grease or spray cookie sheets.

6   Place the dough on a lightly floured pastry cloth or board, and roll out ¼ inch thick. Using a 2-inch round cookie cutter, cut out cookies. Using a spatula, transfer the cookies to prepared cookie sheets, spacing them about 1½ inches apart. Gather the scraps, reroll, and cut out more cookies.

7   Mound the topping generously on the cookies and pat firmly in place. Top each cookie with a candied cherry half, cut side down.

8   Bake in the center of the oven until just golden around the edges, 12 to 15 minutes. Let cool on the cookie sheets for 2 minutes, then transfer to wire racks to cool completely.

SAND TARTS

These traditional cookies get their name from their pleasantly sandy-crisp texture. They crisp up as they cool to become delicious wafers.

COOKIE EXCHANGE TIP: Present these cookies in a gaily printed gift box, or wrap the top and bottom of the box separately in handsome gift paper, and put a bow on the top. Place the cookies in the bottom of the box and set the top at an angle.

1 CUP (2 STICKS) UNSALTED BUTTER, AT ROOM TEMPERATURE

1½ CUPS SUGAR

1 LARGE EGG

2 CUPS ALL-PURPOSE FLOUR

1 LARGE EGG WHITE, LIGHTLY BEATEN

1 TEASPOON GROUND CINNAMON

24 TO 26 PECAN QUARTERS FOR GARNISH

1 In a large bowl, with an electric mixer, beat together the butter and 1¼ cups of the sugar on medium speed until light, 2 to 3 minutes. Beat in the egg. On low speed, gradually beat in the flour just until mixed. The dough will be soft.

2 Divide the dough in half. Pat each half into a thick disk and wrap separately in plastic wrap. Refrigerate until firm, at least 1 hour or up to 1 day.

3 Preheat the oven to 350°F. Have ready nonstick cookie sheets.

4 Place 1 dough disk on a lightly floured pastry cloth or board, and roll out about ¼ inch thick. Using a 2-inch round cookie cutter, cut out cookies. Using a spatula, transfer the cookies to the cookie sheets, spacing them about 1⅛ inches apart. Repeat with the second disk. Combine the scraps, reroll, and cut out more cookies.

5 Brush each cookie with the egg white. In a small bowl or cup, stir together the remaining ¼ cup sugar and the cinnamon. Sprinkle the cinnamon sugar evenly over the cookie rounds. Press a pecan piece into the center of each cookie.

6 Bake in the center of the oven until a light golden brown, 8 to 9 minutes. Let cool on the cookie sheets for 2 minutes, then transfer to wire racks to cool completely.

CINNAMON STARS

makes 30 cookies

The dough for these German Christmas cookies, known as *Zimtsterne*, is very fragile, so we recommend this recipe for experienced bakers. If the dough is too soft and sticky, fold in additional ground almonds. If the dough is too crumbly, add water.

COOKIE EXCHANGE TIP: Arrange the cookies on a platter decorated with pine sprigs. Use different-size star cookie cutters for a more interesting presentation.

4 EGG WHITES, AT ROOM TEMPERATURE

3 CUPS SIFTED CONFECTIONERS' SUGAR, PLUS 2 CUPS UNSIFTED FOR ROLLING

2 CUPS GROUND ALMONDS

2 TABLESPOONS FRESH LEMON JUICE

2 TABLESPOONS FINELY GRATED LEMON ZEST

1 TABLESPOON GROUND CINNAMON

⅛ TEASPOON SALT

1 In a large bowl, with an electric mixer, beat the egg whites on high speed until soft peaks form. Gradually add the 3 cups confectioners' sugar, about ¼ cup at a time, and continue to beat until stiff, glossy peaks form, 2 to 3 minutes.

2 Transfer ¼ cup of the meringue to a small bowl, cover, and refrigerate. Using a rubber spatula, fold the almonds, lemon juice, lemon zest, cinnamon, and salt into the meringue remaining in the bowl. Cover with plastic wrap and refrigerate until firm enough to roll, about 1 hour.

3 Preheat the oven to 275°F. Lightly grease or spray 2 cookie sheets, then dust with flour and tap out the excess.

4 Sprinkle a pastry cloth or clean, smooth kitchen towel with the 2 cups confectioners' sugar. Divide the dough into 4 equal portions. Keep 3 portions refrigerated while you roll out 1 portion ¼ inch thick. Using a 3-inch star cutter, cut out cookies. Place on a prepared cookie sheet, spacing them about 2⅝ inches apart. Brush the cookies lightly with the reserved meringue. Repeat with the remaining dough portions. Combine the scraps, reroll, and cut out more cookies.

5 Bake in the center of the oven until firm but not browned, about 30 minutes. Let cool on the cookie sheets for 2 to 3 minutes, then transfer to wire racks to cool completely.

CHOCOLATE RICE CEREAL
ROCKING HORSES

makes
9
cookies

This old-fashioned recipe is a favorite among youngsters—and the young at heart. Brush the cookies with melted chocolate, then decorate them with mini white chocolate chips or red M&M's. Or, dress them up with colorful decorator gel icings.

COOKIE EXCHANGE TIP: Rocking horses are fun, but you can cut this dough into teddy bears, ducks, or other animals—or even other shapes—instead. You can wrap each rocking horse in clear cellophane and secure it in place with red or green ribbon, to turn the cookie into a gift.

3 TABLESPOONS UNSALTED BUTTER OR MARGARINE

1 (10-OUNCE) PACKAGE REGULAR MARSHMALLOWS, OR 4 CUPS MINIATURE MARSHMALLOWS

¾ TEASPOON GROUND CINNAMON

5 CUPS CRISP COCOA RICE CEREAL

12 OUNCES MILK CHOCOLATE, CHOPPED

MINI WHITE CHOCOLATE CHIPS, RED M&M'S, AND/OR DECORATOR GEL ICING FOR DECORATING

1 Butter a 9-by-13-inch baking pan.

2 In a large, heavy saucepan, melt the butter over low heat. Add the marshmallows and cinnamon and stir until the marshmallows are completely melted. Remove from the heat. Stir in the cereal until evenly coated.

3 Transfer the cereal mixture to the prepared pan. Using the back of a spoon, press evenly over the bottom. Let stand until firm and completely cool, about 15 minutes.

4 Meanwhile, place the milk chocolate in a microwave-safe bowl or in the top of a double boiler. Microwave at 50 percent power or heat over (not touching) barely simmering water, stirring occasionally, until melted and smooth (see page 67).

5 When the cereal mixture is firm, using a 3-inch rocking horse cutter, cut out cookies. Carefully remove from the pan with a small offset spatula or an icing spatula. Using a pastry brush, brush the cookies with the melted chocolate. Decorate as desired.

BIZCOCHITOS

makes 42 cookies

Traditionally, these anise-scented, not-too-sweet Mexican cookies are made with lard. If you want to follow tradition, substitute 1 cup lard for the shortening and butter.

COOKIE EXCHANGE TIP: Line a platter or a rimmed cookie sheet with painted Mexican tiles and arrange these stars attractively on the tiles.

2⅔ CUPS ALL-PURPOSE FLOUR

1½ TEASPOONS BAKING POWDER

1 TEASPOON ANISEEDS

½ TEASPOON SALT

½ CUP (1 STICK) UNSALTED BUTTER, AT ROOM TEMPERATURE

½ CUP VEGETABLE SHORTENING, AT ROOM TEMPERATURE

⅔ CUP SUGAR

1 LARGE EGG

2 TABLESPOONS ORANGE JUICE

TOPPING

¼ CUP SUGAR

1 TABLESPOON GROUND CINNAMON

1   Preheat the oven to 375°F. Lightly grease or spray cookie sheets.

2   In a medium bowl, whisk together the flour, baking powder, aniseeds, and salt. Set aside.

3   In a large bowl, with an electric mixer, beat together the butter, shortening, and sugar on medium speed until light, about 2 minutes. Beat in the egg and orange juice. On low speed, beat in the flour mixture just until mixed. The dough will be stiff.

4   Divide the dough in half or into thirds. Place 1 portion on a lightly floured pastry cloth or board, and roll out ⅛ inch thick. Using a 3-inch star cutter, cut out cookies. If the dough gets too soft and sticky to roll, refrigerate it for 15 to 30 minutes and try again. Using a spatula, place the cookies on a prepared cookie sheet, spacing them about 1⅛ inches apart. Repeat with the remaining dough portion(s). Combine the scraps, reroll, and cut out more cookies.

5   Prepare the topping. In a small bowl, stir together the sugar and cinnamon. Sprinkle the cookies generously with the cinnamon-sugar mixture.

6   Bake in the center of the oven until the edges just begin to turn golden, about 10 minutes. Let cool on the cookie sheets for 2 minutes, then transfer to wire racks to cool completely.

CHAPTER
4

SLICE-AND-BAKE COOKIES

Most slice-and-bake cookies are also refrigerator cookies. And many of the doughs that you roll out and cut, such as those in Rolled and Cutout Cookies (page 149), can also be shaped into a log or a rectangular block and sliced. The refrigerator cookie is more convenient; the cookie cut from rolled dough is more elegant.

You can also mix slightly chunkier ingredients into the dough for sliced and baked cookies, such as raisins, chopped nuts, or candied fruits. Plus, once the dough is molded, you can usually refrigerate it for a few days or freeze it for a few weeks, so you can cut and bake a batch of cookies when you need it.

The doughs for most refrigerator cookies are easy to assemble, slice, and bake. Here are some tips for shaping and storing the dough:

1. Refrigerator cookie dough can usually be wrapped well and frozen for up to a month. Let it thaw in the refrigerator before slicing.

2. When shaping the dough into a log, you can sometimes use the plastic wrap, waxed paper, or foil you will be wrapping it in to help shape it. If necessary, sprinkle the wrap with a bit of flour.

3. If the dough is too sticky to mold into a log, refrigerate it for 30 to 40 minutes, then shape it.

4. To make more interesting cookies, mold the log into a square or a triangle. Or, use the handle of a wooden spoon to make indentations in the log.

5. You can roll the dough log in chopped nuts or colored decorating sugar to give your cookies an interesting edge.

GLACÉ CHERRY

HOLIDAY SLICES

makes 25 cookies

The thin, crisp cookie slices studded with candied, or glacé, fruits will make you think of stained glass. This recipe can easily be doubled.

COOKIE EXCHANGE TIP: For a more festive look, tie 2 or 3 of these cookies together with ribbon.

3 LARGE EGG WHITES

½ CUP SUGAR

1 CUP SIFTED ALL-PURPOSE FLOUR

⅓ CUP SLICED ALMONDS, PREFERABLY TOASTED (SEE PAGE 38)

⅓ CUP CHOPPED PISTACHIOS

⅓ CUP CHOPPED CANDIED PINEAPPLE

¼ CUP CANDIED RED CHERRIES, CHOPPED

¼ CUP CANDIED GREEN CHERRIES, CHOPPED

1 Preheat the oven to 350°F. Lightly grease or spray an 8-inch square pan.

2 In a large bowl, with an electric mixer, beat the egg whites on high speed until soft peaks form. Sprinkle the sugar over the egg whites and continue beating on high speed until the sugar is incorporated. Sprinkle with the flour and beat until incorporated. Stir in the almonds, pistachios, pineapple, and red and green cherries. The batter will be thick. Spoon the batter into the prepared pan and smooth the top.

3 Bake in the center of the oven until golden brown on top and firm to a light touch, 35 to 40 minutes. Let cool completely on a wire rack.

4 Carefully invert the pan onto a work surface. Wrap the cookie block in plastic wrap and refrigerate for 1 day.

5 Preheat the oven to 350°F. Have ready a nonstick cookie sheet.

6 Using a sharp knife, carefully cut the cookie block into ¼-inch-thick slices. Place the slices on the cookie sheet.

7 Bake in the center of the oven until crisp, 5 to 10 minutes. Let cool completely on the cookie sheet on a wire rack.

TO:
SANTA

CHOCOLATE-CHERRY
RIBBON COOKIES

The candied cherries create a jewel-like stripe sandwiched between chocolate. These refrigerator cookies are good to prepare when you will be home all day. They require two chilling periods but are well worth the time.

COOKIE EXCHANGE TIP: Pick up the ribbon motif by serving these in a basket with a wide, tricolor ribbon bow.

2½ CUPS ALL-PURPOSE FLOUR

1½ TEASPOONS BAKING POWDER

½ TEASPOON SALT

1 CUP (2 STICKS) UNSALTED BUTTER, AT ROOM TEMPERATURE

1½ CUPS SUGAR

1 LARGE EGG

2 TEASPOONS VANILLA EXTRACT

½ CUP CANDIED RED OR GREEN CHERRIES, DICED

1 OUNCE UNSWEETENED BAKING CHOCOLATE, MELTED AND COOLED

MILK FOR BRUSHING, HEATED AND COOLED

1   In a medium bowl, whisk together the flour, baking powder, and salt. Set aside.

2   In a large bowl, with an electric mixer, beat together the butter and sugar on medium speed until light, 2 to 3 minutes. Beat in the egg and vanilla. On low speed, gradually beat in the flour mixture just until mixed. The dough will be stiff.

3   Divide the dough into 2 portions, one twice as large as the other. Place the smaller portion in a bowl and stir in the cherries. Shape the cherry dough into a bar 9 inches long and ¾ inch thick. Mix the cooled chocolate into the remaining dough. Divide the chocolate dough in half, and shape each half into a 9-by-1⅜-inch bar the same width as the cherry bar. Wrap each bar separately in plastic wrap and refrigerate until firm, about 2 hours.

4   Unwrap all the bars. Using a pastry brush, brush both sides of the cherry bar with the milk. Sandwich the cherry bar between the 2 chocolate bars, and lightly press the layers together. Wrap the sandwiched layers in fresh plastic wrap and chill until firm, about 2 hours.

5 Preheat the oven to 350°F. Have ready ungreased cookie sheets.

6 Using a small, sharp knife, carefully cut the layered dough block crosswise into ¼-inch-thick slices. Place the cookies on the cookie sheets, spacing them about ½ inch apart (they do not spread).

7 Bake in the center of the oven until just firm to the touch, about 10 minutes. Let cool on the cookie sheets for 2 minutes, then transfer to a wire rack to cool completely.

PISTACHIO AND
CRANBERRY BISCOTTI

makes
40
biscotti

Shelling pistachios is a lot of work. Fortunately, you can find shelled pistachios in some warehouse clubs, natural foods stores, and Middle Eastern markets.

COOKIE EXCHANGE TIP: The green cast of the pistachios and the ruby red of the cranberries give these biscotti true holiday appeal. If you cannot find or don't like pistachios, walnuts or other nuts can be substituted. These cookies will keep in an airtight tin at room temperature for up to a week, so you can bake them well ahead of the party.

3 CUPS ALL-PURPOSE FLOUR

2 TEASPOONS BAKING POWDER

½ TEASPOON SALT, OR ¼ TEASPOON IF USING SALTED PISTACHIOS

1 CUP SUGAR

3 LARGE EGGS

4 TABLESPOONS (½ STICK) UNSALTED BUTTER, MELTED AND SLIGHTLY COOLED

1 TEASPOON VANILLA EXTRACT

½ TEASPOON ORANGE EXTRACT

1 CUP PISTACHIOS, PREFERABLY UNSALTED, COARSELY CHOPPED

1 CUP DRIED CRANBERRIES, COARSELY CHOPPED

1   Preheat the oven to 350°F. Line a large cookie sheet with parchment paper or aluminum foil. If using foil, lightly grease or spray it.

2   In a medium bowl, whisk together the flour, baking powder, and salt. Set aside.

3   In a large bowl, with an electric mixer, beat together the sugar and eggs on high speed until pale yellow. On medium speed, beat in the butter and the vanilla and orange extracts. On low speed, beat in the flour mixture just until mixed. Stir in the pistachios and cranberries. The dough will be medium-stiff.

4   Spoon the dough onto the prepared baking sheet in 2 strips, each about 12 inches long. With wet or floured fingers, pat each strip into a log about 3 inches wide and taller in the center than at the edges. Refrigerate until firm, about 20 minutes.

continued...

. . . *continued*

5 Bake in the center of the oven until lightly browned and nearly firm to the touch, about 30 minutes. Let cool on the cookie sheet on a wire rack for 30 minutes, then carefully transfer the logs to a cutting board, using the parchment to help lift them.

6 Reduce the oven temperature to 325°F. Line the cookie sheet with fresh parchment paper or foil.

7 Cut the logs crosswise into ½-inch-thick slices. Place the slices, with a cut side down, on the prepared cookie sheet, spacing them about ¼ inch apart.

8 Bake in the center of the oven until pale gold, about 20 minutes. Let cool completely on the cookie sheet on a wire rack. The biscotti will crisp as they cool.

SEEDY, NUTTY
LITTLE SLICES

makes about
40
cookies

Sprinkle these thin, crisp slices with cinnamon sugar before serving, if desired.

COOKIE EXCHANGE TIP: Wrap 3 cookies together in colored or clear cellophane and tie with white ribbon. This small package is perfect because the thin slices are very rich.

6 LARGE EGG WHITES

1 CUP SUGAR

2 CUPS ALL-PURPOSE FLOUR, SIFTED

⅔ CUP UNSALTED HULLED PUMPKIN SEEDS *(PEPITAS)*

⅔ CUP SHELLED SUNFLOWER SEEDS OR PECANS

⅔ CUP PINE NUTS

⅓ CUP SESAME SEEDS

1   Preheat the oven to 350°F. Lightly grease or spray 2 miniature (5-by-3-by-2-inch) loaf pans.

2   In a large bowl, with an electric mixer, beat the egg whites on high speed until foamy. Add the sugar in a slow, steady stream, beating until the sugar has dissolved and the egg whites are glossy. On low speed, beat in the flour, pumpkin seeds, sunflower seeds, pine nuts, and sesame seeds. The batter will be thick.

3   Divide the batter evenly between the prepared loaf pans. Smooth the tops with the back of a spoon.

4   Bake in the center of the oven until firm to a light touch and just golden, 35 to 40 minutes. Let cool completely in the pans on wire racks.

5   Invert the pans onto a work surface, and lift off the pans. Wrap the "loaves" in aluminum foil and refrigerate for 1 to 2 days.

6   Preheat the oven to 350°F. Have ready ungreased nonstick cookie sheets.

7   Cut the loaves into thin slices (a scant ¼ inch thick). Arrange the cookies flat on the cookie sheets, spacing them about 1 inch apart.

8   Bake in the center of the oven until crisp, about 10 minutes. Let cool on the cookie sheets for 2 minutes, then transfer to wire racks to cool completely.

CHECKERBOARD COOKIES

You can add ⅓ cup ground pistachios to the light dough to give it a nice flavor and slightly green cast.

COOKIE EXCHANGE TIP: For fun, mound the cookies on a checkerboard topped with a sheet of clear cellophane. A stack of checkerboard pieces set near the cookies will complete the effect.

2 CUPS ALL-PURPOSE FLOUR

¼ TEASPOON BAKING POWDER

¾ CUP (1½ STICKS) UNSALTED BUTTER, AT ROOM TEMPERATURE

1½ CUPS SUGAR

2 LARGE EGG YOLKS

2 TABLESPOONS UNSWEETENED COCOA POWDER

3 TABLESPOONS WATER

½ TEASPOON VANILLA EXTRACT

1 LARGE EGG WHITE, LIGHTLY BEATEN WITH 1 TABLESPOON WATER

1 In a medium bowl, whisk together the flour and baking powder. Set aside.

2 In a large bowl, with an electric mixer, beat together the butter and sugar on medium speed until light, 2 to 3 minutes. Beat in the egg yolks. On low speed, gradually beat in the flour mixture just until mixed.

3 Remove half of the dough from the bowl and place in a second bowl. With a wooden spoon, stir the cocoa powder and water into the dough in the original bowl until incorporated. Stir the vanilla into the dough in the second bowl.

4 Roll out the vanilla dough on a lightly floured pastry cloth or board into an 8-by-10-inch rectangle about ⅛ inch thick. Repeat with the chocolate dough.

5   To create a checkerboard pattern, cut six ½-inch-wide strips length-wise from the vanilla dough. Repeat with the chocolate dough. Gather the vanilla dough scraps and roll out to a rectangle about 8 inches wide and ⅛ inch thick. Repeat with the chocolate dough scraps. Lightly brush all of the strips with the egg white and adhere 4 of the strips to one another, edge to edge, alternating chocolate and vanilla doughs. Top with another 4 strips, alternating so a chocolate strip is atop a vanilla strip and vice versa. Repeat to make a third layer. You should have a 2-inch square log. Cut the log in half crosswise to make 2 short logs. Brush the thinly rolled vanilla dough rectangle with egg white and wrap it, egg white side in, around 1 short log, sealing the seam. Repeat with the thinly rolled chocolate dough rectangle and the remaining short log.

6   Wrap each log separately in plastic wrap and refrigerate until firm, at least 1 hour or up to 1 day.

7   Preheat the oven to 375°F. Lightly grease or spray cookie sheets.

8   Using a small, sharp knife, cut each log crosswise into ¼-inch-thick slices. Place the cookies on the prepared cookie sheets, spacing them about 1½ inches apart.

9   Bake in the center of the oven until firm to a light touch and golden on the bottom, 5 to 8 minutes. Let cool on the cookie sheets for 5 minutes, then transfer to wire racks to cool completely.

makes
42
cookies

MOLASSES COOKIES
WITH BUTTER-NUT TOPPING

Most supermarkets carry unsulfured molasses in two varieties: regular and robust (or dark). The regular, or light, variety is the type to use here.

COOKIE EXCHANGE TIP: Adorn a plate of these rich cookies with an old-fashioned German-style nutcracker.

DOUGH

1½ CUPS ALL-PURPOSE FLOUR

¼ TEASPOON BAKING SODA

½ CUP VEGETABLE SHORTENING

3 TABLESPOONS UNSULFURED MOLASSES

1 TEASPOON INSTANT COFFEE CRYSTALS

½ TEASPOON VANILLA EXTRACT

BUTTER-NUT TOPPING

½ CUP (1 STICK) UNSALTED BUTTER, AT ROOM TEMPERATURE

½ CUP CONFECTIONERS' SUGAR

¼ CUP CHOPPED ALMONDS

¼ CUP CHOPPED WALNUTS

1   Prepare the dough. In a medium bowl, sift together the flour and baking soda. Set aside.

2   In a large bowl, with an electric mixer, beat together the shortening and molasses on medium speed until light, about 2 minutes. Beat in the coffee crystals and vanilla. On low speed, beat in the flour mixture just until mixed. The dough will be firm.

3   On a floured board, gather the dough into a ball, then shape into a log about 1 inch in diameter and 13 inches long. Wrap in plastic wrap and refrigerate until firm, at least 2 hours or up to overnight.

4   Prepare the topping. In a food processor, combine the butter, sugar, almonds, and walnuts and process until crumbly and well mixed. (Or, combine the ingredients in a medium bowl and beat with an electric mixer on low speed until combined and crumbly.) Scrape the butter mixture onto a sheet of aluminum foil or plastic wrap and shape into a log about 1 inch in diameter. Wrap it in the foil and freeze for at least 2 hours or up to overnight.

5 Preheat the oven to 350°F. Lightly grease or spray cookie sheets.

6 Using a small, sharp knife, cut the molasses dough into ¼-inch-thick
   slices. Place on the cookie sheets, spacing them about 1½ inches
   apart. Top each cookie with a thin slice of the butter-nut topping.

7 Bake in the center of the oven until firm on top and golden brown
   on the bottom, 10 to 12 minutes. Let cool on the cookie sheets for
   2 minutes, then transfer to wire racks to cool completely.

makes about
48
cookies

MINCEMEAT AND
LEMON COOKIES

Grated lemon zest picks up the citrus peel flavor in the mincemeat and makes a nice counterpoint to the sweet raisins.

COOKIE EXCHANGE TIP: For a nostalgic look, set the plate of cookies on a vintage cake stand. A stand made of milk glass or Depression glass looks especially nice.

3 CUPS SIFTED ALL-PURPOSE FLOUR

½ TEASPOON BAKING SODA

¼ TEASPOON SALT

1 TEASPOON GROUND CINNAMON

¾ CUP (1½ STICKS) UNSALTED BUTTER, AT ROOM TEMPERATURE

1 CUP SUGAR

1 LARGE EGG

½ TEASPOON VANILLA EXTRACT

2 TEASPOONS FINELY GRATED LEMON ZEST

¾ CUP PREPARED MINCEMEAT

½ CUP CHOPPED PECANS OR WALNUTS, PREFERABLY TOASTED (SEE PAGE 38)

1 In a medium bowl, sift together the flour, baking soda, salt, and cinnamon. Set aside.

2 In a large bowl, with an electric mixer, beat together the butter and sugar on medium speed until light, about 2 minutes. Beat in the egg, vanilla, and lemon zest. Stir in the mincemeat. On low speed, gradually beat in the flour mixture just until mixed. Stir in the nuts. The dough will be stiff.

3 Divide the dough in half. Knead each half on a lightly floured pastry cloth or board until easy to handle. Shape each half into a log about 1⅓ inches in diameter and 12 inches long.

4 Wrap each log in aluminum foil or plastic wrap and refrigerate until firm, several hours or up to overnight.

5 Preheat the oven to 375°F. Have ready ungreased nonstick cookie sheets.

6 Using a small, sharp knife, cut the logs into slices ⅛ to ¼ inch thick. Place the cookies on the cookie sheets, spacing them about 1⅓ inches apart.

7 Bake in the center of the oven until just firm to the touch, 8 to 10 minutes. Let cool on the cookie sheets for 3 to 5 minutes, then transfer to wire racks to cool completely.

LIME-PISTACHIO THINS

makes
60
cookies

For a more interesting flavor, use four Key limes instead of the regular limes.

COOKIE EXCHANGE TIP: Pistachios and lime zest give these thin wafers a green cast that is nicely set off by a red tray or plate.

2 CUPS ALL-PURPOSE FLOUR

¼ TEASPOON SALT

1 CUP (2 STICKS) UNSALTED BUTTER, AT ROOM TEMPERATURE

1 CUP SUGAR

2 LARGE EGGS

FINELY GRATED ZEST AND JUICE FROM 2 LIMES

1 LARGE EGG WHITE, LIGHTLY BEATEN

1 CUP FINELY CHOPPED PISTACHIOS, PECANS, OR WALNUTS, PREFERABLY TOASTED (SEE PAGE 38)

1 In a medium bowl, whisk together the flour and salt. Set aside.

2 In a large bowl, with an electric mixer, beat together the butter and sugar on medium speed until light, 2 to 3 minutes. Beat in the eggs, one at a time, mixing well after each addition. Beat in the lime zest and juice. On low speed, gradually beat in the flour mixture just until mixed. The dough will be soft and sticky.

3 Divide the dough in half. Scrape each half onto a sheet of floured aluminum foil or plastic wrap. With wet hands, or using the foil or plastic wrap, shape each half into a square log about 2½ inches wide and 15 inches long.

4 Wrap each log in the foil and refrigerate until firm, about 1 hour.

5 Unwrap the dough logs, brush them with the egg white, and roll them in the nuts. Rewrap them and refrigerate until very firm, about 1 hour.

6 Preheat the oven to 375°F. Lightly grease or spray cookie sheets.

7 Using a small, sharp knife, cut the logs into ¼-inch-thick slices. Place on the prepared cookie sheets, spacing them about 1⅛ inches apart.

8 Bake in the center of the oven until just beginning to turn golden, 8 to 10 minutes. Let cool on the cookie sheets for 2 to 3 minutes, then transfer to wire racks to cool completely.

CHAPTER
5

FILLED COOKIES

A good cookie attains greatness when you add a luscious filling to it. Nearly every culture that bakes cookies has given us at least one classic filled cookie, from Swedish thumbprint cookies and Polish poppy-seed cookies to American vanilla-filled sandwich cookies. Here, you'll find ideas for specific fillings, but don't be limited by what's in a recipe. Let your creativity guide you to whatever sounds good, such as using guava paste or mango butter in place of vanilla icing for a taste of the tropics.

The easiest filled cookies call for spreading a luscious buttercream or other filling on the bottom of one thin wafer and topping it with a second thin wafer, bottom side down. Filling a yeast horn or a bear paw requires a bit more finesse. Here are some tips for making the best filled cookies:

1. Don't overfill sandwich cookies. If you use too much icing, it will squeeze out the sides when you bite into it.

2. For the best-looking sandwich cookies, make the cookies as uniform as possible so they stack up neatly.

3. Don't overfill turnover-style or crescent-style cookies, or the dough may tear.

4. Unless you're freezing them, don't store crisp cookies with moist fillings in airtight containers, which can soften them and make them gummy. Keep them in a cool, dry place.

VANILLA
SANDWICH COOKIES

makes
24
sandwich
cookies

Don't be in a rush to put these on the table. Allow time for the frosting to set before serving.

COOKIE EXCHANGE TIP: Vary the filling according to your own taste. Use jam, peanut butter, chocolate frosting, or even guava paste.

BASIC BUTTER COOKIES DOUGH (PAGE 150)

VANILLA BUTTERCREAM (PAGE 17)

SIFTED CONFECTIONERS' SUGAR FOR DUSTING

1 Make the butter cookies dough and refrigerate as directed.

2 Preheat the oven to 350°F. Lightly grease or spray cookie sheets.

3 Place the dough on a lightly floured pastry cloth or board, and roll out ⅛ inch thick. Using a 2-inch round cookie cutter, cut out cookies. Using a spatula, transfer to the prepared cookie sheets, spacing them about 1½ inches apart. Gather the scraps, reroll, and cut out more cookies.

4 Bake in the center of the oven until faintly golden, 6 to 8 minutes. Let cool on the cookie sheets for 1 minute, then transfer to wire racks to cool completely.

5 Turn half of the cookies bottom side up. Using a small knife or icing spatula, spread the bottoms with the buttercream, using about 1 tablespoon for each cookie. Top with the remaining cookies, bottom side down. Dust the tops with sifted confectioners' sugar.

CHOCOLATE SANDWICH COOKIES WITH

MARSHMALLOW-MINT FILLING

makes **24** sandwich cookies

Make a double batch of these tasty sandwich cookies because they disappear fast. Youngsters especially like the chocolate-marshmallow combination.

COOKIE EXCHANGE TIP: Instead of filling these cookies, place 1 large marshmallow on top of each cookie. Melt 1 (12-ounce) package semisweet chocolate chips (about 2 cups) with 1 tablespoon light corn syrup and let cool slightly. Using a pastry brush, cover the marshmallows with the chocolate. Makes 48 cookies.

1¾ CUPS ALL-PURPOSE FLOUR

½ TEASPOON BAKING SODA

½ CUP UNSWEETENED COCOA POWDER

½ CUP UNSALTED BUTTER OR VEGETABLE SHORTENING, AT ROOM TEMPERATURE

1 CUP FIRMLY PACKED DARK BROWN SUGAR

1 LARGE EGG

1 TEASPOON VANILLA EXTRACT

½ CUP MILK

1 Preheat the oven to 350°F. Lightly grease or spray nonstick cookie sheets.

2 In a medium bowl, sift together the flour, baking soda, and cocoa powder. Set aside.

3 In a large bowl, with an electric mixer, beat the butter on medium speed until light, about 2 minutes. Add the brown sugar and beat until fluffy, about 2 minutes. Beat in the egg and vanilla. On low speed, beat in the flour mixture in 2 additions alternately with the milk, beginning and ending with the flour mixture, just until mixed.

4 Drop the batter by rounded teaspoons onto the prepared cookie sheets, spacing them about 2 inches apart.

continued...

. . . continued

FILLING

½ CUP CRUSHED GREEN OR RED MINT-FLAVORED HARD CANDIES

½ CUP CONFECTIONERS' SUGAR

4 TABLESPOONS (½ STICK) UNSALTED BUTTER, AT ROOM TEMPERATURE

1 CUP MARSHMALLOW CREME

1 TEASPOON PEPPERMINT EXTRACT

5 Bake in the center of the oven until firm to the touch, 13 to 15 minutes. Let cool on the cookie sheets for 1 minute, then transfer to wire racks to cool completely.

6 While the cookies are cooling, prepare the filling. In a food processor, combine the crushed candies, confectioners' sugar, butter, marshmallow creme, and peppermint extract. Process for only a few seconds, just until the ingredients are combined.

7 Turn half of the cookies bottom side up. Using a small knife or an icing spatula, swirl the filling on the bottoms, using 1 rounded teaspoon for each cookie. Top with the remaining cookies, bottom side down.

SOFT SANDWICH COOKIES

makes about 24 sandwich cookies

If you like Linzer torte, you will like these cookies. The dough is very close in flavor to Linzer dough and the filling is raspberry jam, which is also used in the famous torte. You can substitute a jam of your choice; orange marmalade is good.

COOKIE EXCHANGE TIP: These cookies are soft, so be careful when handling them and never stack them. Instead, arrange in a single layer on a serving tray.

⅓ CUP (5½ TABLESPOONS) UNSALTED BUTTER, AT ROOM TEMPERATURE

1 CUP GROUND ALMONDS

1 CUP ALL-PURPOSE FLOUR

3 TABLESPOONS GRANULATED SUGAR

1 TEASPOON UNSWEETENED COCOA POWDER

1 TEASPOON VANILLA EXTRACT

¼ CUP SEEDLESS RASPBERRY JAM

SIFTED CONFECTIONERS' SUGAR FOR DUSTING

1 Preheat the oven to 350°F. Lightly grease or spray cookie sheets.

2 In a large bowl, with an electric mixer, beat the butter on medium speed until smooth. On low speed, beat in the almonds, flour, granulated sugar, cocoa, and vanilla. The dough should be soft but easy to handle. If it is too sticky, refrigerate it for 15 to 30 minutes.

3 Pinch off pieces of the dough and roll between your palms into balls about 1 inch in diameter. Place on the prepared cookie sheets, spacing them about 1½ inches apart. Lightly flatten the balls with the bottom of a drinking glass.

4 Bake in the center of the oven until firm to the touch and just beginning to turn golden around the edges, about 10 minutes. Let the cookies cool on the cookie sheets for 2 minutes, then transfer them to wire racks to cool completely.

5 Turn half of the cookies bottom side up. Using a small knife, spread the bottoms with the jam, using about ½ teaspoon for each cookie. Top with the remaining cookies, bottom side down. Dust the tops with sifted confectioners' sugar.

TWO-BITE

OATMEAL SANDWICH COOKIES WITH
NUTELLA FILLING

Nutella, which originated in northwest Italy, is a sweet spread made from hazel-nuts, cocoa powder, skim milk, and sugar. It is sold in 13-ounce jars in specialty foods shops and well-stocked supermarkets.

COOKIE EXCHANGE TIP: Fill a Christmas stocking about half full with tissue paper. Line the rest of the stocking with waxed paper or plastic wrap and fill with cookies.

2½ CUPS QUICK-COOKING (NOT INSTANT) ROLLED OATS

1¾ CUPS ALL-PURPOSE FLOUR

1 TEASPOON BAKING POWDER

¾ TEASPOON GROUND CINNAMON

½ TEASPOON GROUND CLOVES

1 CUP (2 STICKS) UNSALTED BUTTER, AT ROOM TEMPERATURE

½ CUP GRANULATED SUGAR

½ CUP FIRMLY PACKED LIGHT BROWN SUGAR

2 LARGE EGGS

1 TEASPOON VANILLA EXTRACT

1 CUP DRIED CURRANTS

ABOUT ½ CUP NUTELLA

1 Preheat the oven to 375°F. Lightly grease or spray cookie sheets.

2 Put the oats in a food processor and process until ground. Set aside.

3 In a medium bowl, whisk together the flour, baking powder, cinnamon, and cloves. Set aside.

4 In a large bowl, with an electric mixer, beat together the butter and granulated and brown sugars on medium speed until light, 2 to 3 minutes. Beat in the eggs, one at a time, beating well after each addition, and then add the vanilla. On low speed, gradually beat in the flour mixture just until mixed. Stir in the oats and currants. The dough will be firm.

5 Drop the dough by heaping teaspoons onto the prepared cookie sheets, spacing them about 1½ inches apart.

6 Bake in the center of the oven until lightly golden and firm to the touch, 12 to 15 minutes. Let cool on the cookie sheets for 3 to 5 minutes, then transfer to wire racks to cool completely.

7 Turn half of the cookies bottom side up. Using a small knife, spread the bottoms with the Nutella, using about 1 teaspoon for each cookie. Top with the remaining cookies, bottom side down. Press the cookies together so they stick to each other and the Nutella spreads to the edges with just a small amount of the filling showing.

KOLACKY

Various Central European countries have their own variations on these popular filled cookies, sometimes spelled *kolache* or *kolace*. Some are made with a yeast dough, others with cream cheese or even ice cream. The cream cheese dough is the most popular for the Polish version of these rich cookies.

COOKIE EXCHANGE TIP: The sweet fillings of kolacky peek through the golden dough and resemble beautiful stained glass windows in a cathedral. Play up this resemblance by using different fillings and arranging the cookies on a tray in a starburst pattern.

6 OUNCES (ABOUT ¾ CUP) CREAM CHEESE, AT ROOM TEMPERATURE

1 CUP (2 STICKS) UNSALTED BUTTER, AT ROOM TEMPERATURE

1 TABLESPOON GRANULATED SUGAR

2½ CUPS ALL-PURPOSE FLOUR

ABOUT ¾ CUP PREPARED POPPY-SEED, APRICOT, OR PRUNE FILLING OR THICK JAM OF CHOICE

SIFTED CONFECTIONERS' SUGAR FOR DUSTING

1 In a large bowl, with an electric mixer, beat together the cream cheese, butter, and granulated sugar on medium speed until light, about 2 minutes. On low speed, gradually beat in the flour just until mixed. The dough will be soft and sticky.

2 Divide the dough in half. Pat each half into a thick disk and wrap separately in plastic wrap. Refrigerate until firm enough to handle, at least 1 hour or up to 1 day.

3 Preheat the oven to 350°F. Lightly grease or spray cookie sheets.

4 Dust a pastry cloth or board with flour or confectioners' sugar. Remove 1 dough disk from the refrigerator and place it on the pastry cloth. Keep the remaining dough disk refrigerated. Roll out the dough into a square or rectangle ⅛ inch thick. Cut into 2½-inch squares.

continued...

. . . continued

5   Place 1 teaspoon of the filling in the center of each square. Pull
    2 opposite corners of the square into the middle, and pinch the edges
    together to seal. Place the cookies on the prepared cookie sheets,
    spacing them about 1⅛ inches apart. Repeat with the remaining dough
    and filling.

6   Bake in the center of the oven until lightly golden, 12 to 15 minutes.
    Let cool on the cookie sheets for 1 to 2 minutes, then transfer to wire
    racks. Dust the tops with sifted confectioners' sugar while still warm,
    then let cool completely.

BEAR PAWS

These cookies are folded over, then slit in four places, so the resulting cookie resembles a large paw. If the jam is a bit too cool to brush easily, warm it for 10 to 15 seconds in the microwave at 50 percent power.

COOKIE EXCHANGE TIP: These large cookies are worth 2 or 3 smaller cookies in exchange. For fun, sit a teddy bear by a plateful of the cookies.

3 CUPS ALL-PURPOSE FLOUR

¼ CUP UNSWEETENED COCOA POWDER

1 TEASPOON BAKING SODA

½ TEASPOON BAKING POWDER

⅛ TEASPOON SALT

½ TEASPOON GROUND CINNAMON

1 CUP (2 STICKS) UNSALTED BUTTER, AT ROOM TEMPERATURE

2 CUPS GRANULATED SUGAR

2 LARGE EGGS

¼ CUP SEEDLESS RASPBERRY JAM

¼ CUP FINELY CHOPPED PECANS OR WALNUTS

¼ CUP CONFECTIONERS' SUGAR

1 Preheat the oven to 375°F. Lightly grease or spray cookie sheets.

2 In a large bowl, whisk together the flour, cocoa, baking soda, baking powder, salt, and cinnamon. Set aside.

3 In a large bowl, with an electric mixer, beat together the butter and granulated sugar on medium speed until light, about 3 minutes. Beat in the eggs. On low speed, gradually beat in the flour mixture just until mixed. The dough will be medium firm.

4 Place the dough on a lightly floured pastry cloth or board, and roll out into a 12-inch square. Using a 3-inch round cookie cutter, cut out circles. Gather the scraps, reroll, and cut out more circles.

5 Brush the circles evenly with the jam, stopping short of the edges, and sprinkle evenly with the nuts. Fold each circle in half, and press the edges to secure closed. Cut 4 evenly spaced ½-inch-long slits on the round side of each half circle. Place on the prepared cookie sheets, spacing them about 1½ inches apart. Sift the confectioners' sugar evenly over the tops.

6 Bake in the center of the oven just until the cookies spring back when lightly touched, 8 to 10 minutes. These cookies firm up as they cool, so do not overbake. Let cool on the cookie sheets for 2 to 3 minutes, then transfer to wire racks to cool completely.

SWEDISH
THUMBPRINT COOKIES

makes about
30
cookies

Lingonberries are wild relatives of the cranberry. If you cannot find lingonberry jam or jelly (available in some specialty foods shops and well-stocked super-markets), jellied cranberry sauce or currant jelly makes a good substitute.

You can fill thumbprint cookies before baking, as we do here, or after baking (see Pine Nut Thumbprint Cookies with Fig Jam, page 194). Jam or jelly softens during baking, so if you fill the cookies before baking, be sure to center the indentation carefully, or the jelly will run down the side of the cookie.

COOKIE EXCHANGE TIP: The deep red filling of these Swedish favorites looks lovely against a forest green plate. Add some snippets of gold fabric ribbon for even more elegance.

1 CUP (2 STICKS) UNSALTED BUTTER, AT ROOM TEMPERATURE

½ CUP SUGAR

2 LARGE EGG YOLKS

1 TEASPOON VANILLA EXTRACT

¼ TEASPOON SALT

2 CUPS ALL-PURPOSE FLOUR

1 LARGE EGG WHITE, LIGHTLY BEATEN (OPTIONAL)

½ CUP FINELY CHOPPED WALNUTS OR ALMONDS

ABOUT ⅓ CUP LINGONBERRY JAM OR JELLY

1   Preheat the oven to 350°F. Lightly grease or spray cookie sheets.

2   In a large bowl, with an electric mixer, beat together the butter and sugar on medium speed until light, about 2 minutes. Beat in the egg yolks, vanilla, and salt. On low speed, beat in the flour until a fairly stiff dough forms. The dough should be pliable but not sticky. If it is too sticky, refrigerate it for 15 to 30 minutes.

3   Pinch off pieces of the dough and roll between your palms into balls about 1 inch in diameter. Roll each ball in the egg white (this is optional, but it helps the nuts to adhere better), then in the nuts, coating evenly. Place on the prepared cookie sheets, spacing them about 1½ inches apart.

4 With your thumb, make an indentation in the center of each cookie. Fill each indentation with about ½ teaspoon jam.

5 Bake in the center of the oven until golden, about 15 minutes. Let cool on the cookie sheets for 2 minutes, then transfer to wire racks to cool completely.

PINE NUT

THUMBPRINT COOKIES WITH FIG JAM

makes about 48 cookies

Let your child fill the indentations on the cooled cookies with jam. It can be a lot of fun. In the past, bakers often used wooden clothespins to make the indentation in the cookie. Nowadays, most clothespins are plastic, but they still work for creating a nice hollow in the dough.

COOKIE EXCHANGE TIP: Play up the pine nut theme by arranging the cookies on a forest green platter and surrounding them with glitter-dusted pinecones.

1 CUP (2 STICKS) UNSALTED BUTTER, AT ROOM TEMPERATURE

½ CUP SUGAR

⅓ CUP HONEY

1 TEASPOON VANILLA EXTRACT

2½ CUPS ALL-PURPOSE FLOUR

1¼ CUPS FINELY CHOPPED PINE NUTS, WALNUTS, OR PISTACHIOS

ABOUT ½ CUP FIG JAM OR JAM OF CHOICE

1   Preheat the oven to 350°F. Lightly grease or spray cookie sheets.

2   In a large bowl, with an electric mixer, beat together the butter, sugar, honey, and vanilla on medium speed until light, about 2 minutes. On low speed, gradually beat in the flour just until mixed. Stir in 1 cup of the nuts. The dough will be stiff.

3   Pinch off pieces of the dough and roll between your palms into walnut-sized balls. Place on the prepared cookie sheets, spacing them about 1½ inches apart.

4   Bake in the center of the oven until firm to the touch and just golden on the bottom, about 10 minutes. Let cool slightly, then make an indentation in the center of each cookie using your thumb, the handle of a large wooden spoon, or a clothespin. Transfer to wire racks to cool completely.

5   Fill the indentation in each cookie with about ½ teaspoon of the jam. Then sprinkle the jam-filled centers evenly with the remaining nuts.

CHOCOLATE
PEANUT BUTTER CUPS

makes 24 cookies

This is the cookie equivalent of the popular peanut butter cup candy.

COOKIE EXCHANGE TIP: For a fancier cookie, sprinkle some chopped peanuts over the filling before baking, or drizzle the cookies with melted milk chocolate after baking. The cookies also look nice set in gold metallic cupcake liners.

CRUST

1¼ CUPS ALL-PURPOSE FLOUR

¼ CUP UNSWEETENED COCOA POWDER

¾ CUP CONFECTIONERS' SUGAR

¼ TEASPOON SALT

½ CUP (1 STICK) UNSALTED BUTTER, AT ROOM TEMPERATURE

1 LARGE EGG YOLK

1 TO 2 TABLESPOONS COLD MILK OR HEAVY CREAM, OR AS NEEDED

FILLING

1 CUP CREAMY PEANUT BUTTER, AT ROOM TEMPERATURE

1 CUP PLUS 2 TABLESPOONS CONFECTIONERS' SUGAR

1 TEASPOON VANILLA EXTRACT

1 LARGE EGG

1   Prepare the crust. In a medium bowl, whisk together the flour, cocoa powder, confectioners' sugar, and salt. Set aside.

2   In a large bowl, with an electric mixer, beat the butter on medium speed until light, about 2 minutes. Beat in the egg yolk. On low speed, beat in the flour mixture just until mixed. Then beat in enough milk to make a medium-stiff, fairly sticky dough.

3   Gather the dough into a ball, pat into a thick disk, and wrap in plastic wrap. Refrigerate until firm enough to roll easily, 1 to 2 hours.

4   Lightly grease or spray 24 mini muffin cups.

5   Place the dough disk on a floured pastry cloth or board, and roll out ⅛ inch thick. Using a 2⅛-inch round cookie cutter, cut out rounds. Gently ease each dough round into a prepared muffin cup, pressing gently against the bottom and sides to create an indentation. Refrigerate for 20 to 30 minutes.

6   Meanwhile, prepare the filling. In a food processor, combine the peanut butter, confectioners' sugar, vanilla, and egg and process until a smooth, soft, sticky doughlike mixture forms. Or, combine the ingredients in a medium bowl and beat with an electric mixer on medium speed until the doughlike mixture forms.

continued . . .

. . . continued

7 Gather the filling into a ball and wrap in plastic wrap. Refrigerate until firm enough to handle, 20 to 30 minutes. While the filling chills, preheat the oven to 375°F.

8 Remove the dough cups from the refrigerator. Pinch off pieces of the filling and roll between your palms into balls a bit smaller than 1 inch. Place a ball in each dough cup, and flatten slightly with a fingertip.

9 Bake in the center of the oven for 15 minutes. The filling should look puffy, and when you carefully insert a bread knife between a chocolate cup and the pan, the cup should loosen easily from the pan. Let cool in the pan for 10 to 15 minutes, then gently pry the chocolate cups out of the muffin pan with a bread knife. Let cool completely on wire racks.

CINNAMON-NUT HORNS

makes
36
cookies

This is an interesting cookie because yeast is added to the dough, which enhances the lightness and flavor of this cookie. The dough must rest overnight.

COOKIE EXCHANGE TIP: For an elegant display, arrange these cookies on a silver tray.

DOUGH

3 CUPS ALL-PURPOSE FLOUR

1 (¼-OUNCE) PACKAGE ACTIVE DRY YEAST

1 CUP (2 STICKS) UNSALTED BUTTER, AT ROOM TEMPERATURE

3 LARGE EGG YOLKS

1 CUP SOUR CREAM

2 CUPS GRANULATED SUGAR

½ CUP GROUND CINNAMON

1 (10-OUNCE) JAR RED CURRANT JELLY OR SEEDLESS RASPBERRY JAM (ABOUT ⅞ CUP)

1¼ CUPS FINELY CHOPPED PECANS, HAZELNUTS, OR WALNUTS, PREFERABLY TOASTED (SEE PAGE 38)

1 CUP DRIED CURRANTS

DECORATING SUGAR FOR SPRINKLING (OPTIONAL)

1 In a medium bowl, whisk together the flour and yeast. Set aside. In a large bowl, with an electric mixer, beat the butter on medium speed until light, about 2 minutes. Beat in the egg yolks and sour cream. On low speed, gradually beat in the flour mixture just until mixed. Gather the dough into a ball and wrap in plastic wrap. Refrigerate overnight.

2 Preheat the oven to 350°F. Have ready nonstick cookie sheets, or line regular cookie sheets with parchment paper.

3 In a medium bowl, stir together the granulated sugar and cinnamon.

4 Divide the dough into 3 equal portions. Sprinkle about ¼ cup of the cinnamon sugar over a clean, smooth towel. Place 1 dough portion on the prepared cloth, and roll out into a circle about 2½ inches in diameter and ⅛ to ¼ inch thick. Gently spread one-third of the jam evenly over the dough. Sprinkle one-third each of the nuts and currants evenly over the jam. With a small, sharp knife, cut the dough into 12 equal wedges. Starting from the wide end, roll up each wedge toward the center, then curl the ends in slightly to form a crescent. Sprinkle the crescents generously with additional cinnamon sugar, then place them on the cookie sheets, spacing them about 1½ inches apart. Repeat with the 2 remaining dough portions, sprinkling the pastry cloth with ¼ cup cinnamon sugar before rolling each portion.

5 Sprinkle lightly with the decorating sugar, if desired. Bake in the center of the oven until the cookies are just firm to a light touch and golden, 14 to 15 minutes. Let cool on the cookie sheets for 3 minutes, then transfer to wire racks to cool completely.

makes 30 cookies

ROLLED COCONUT-
STRAWBERRY COOKIES

Before baking, brush the cookies with melted butter. This enhances the flavor and helps the cookies to brown lightly. You can substitute dried currants or small chocolate chips for the coconut.

COOKIE EXCHANGE TIP: These melt-in-the-mouth cookies are popular, so you may want to double the recipe. Wrap them in colored cellophane tied with complementary ribbons for a pretty presentation.

DOUGH

1 (8-OUNCE) PACKAGE CREAM
CHEESE, AT ROOM TEMPERATURE

1 CUP (2 STICKS) UNSALTED BUTTER,
AT ROOM TEMPERATURE

2 CUPS ALL-PURPOSE FLOUR

FILLING

2 CUPS SWEETENED SHREDDED
OR FLAKED COCONUT

1 CUP GROUND WALNUTS
OR ALMONDS

1 TABLESPOON GROUND CINNAMON

2 TABLESPOONS SUGAR

1 (12-OUNCE) JAR STRAWBERRY
JAM OR SEEDLESS RASPBERRY JAM
(ABOUT 1 CUP)

4 TABLESPOONS UNSALTED BUTTER,
MELTED

1 Prepare the dough. In a large bowl, with an electric mixer, beat together the cream cheese and butter on medium speed until light and creamy, about 2 minutes. On low speed, beat in the flour, 1 cup at a time. The dough will be sticky.

2 Divide the dough into 3 equal portions. Pat each into a thick disk and wrap separately in plastic wrap. Refrigerate until firm, at least 2 hours or up to overnight. Bring the dough to cool room temperature before rolling.

3 Preheat the oven to 375°F. Lightly grease or spray cookie sheets.

4 Prepare the filling. In a medium bowl, stir together the coconut, nuts, cinnamon, and sugar.

5   Place 1 dough disk on a lightly floured pastry cloth or board, and roll out into a circle 10 to 12 inches in diameter and ⅛ to ¼ inch thick. Gently spread one-third of the jam evenly over the dough. Sprinkle one-third of the coconut mixture evenly over the jam. With a small, sharp knife or a pizza cutter, cut the dough into 10 equal wedges. Starting from the wide end, roll up each wedge toward the center, then curl the ends in slightly to form a crescent. Place the crescents on the prepared cookie sheets, spacing them about 1⅛ inches apart. Repeat with the 2 remaining dough portions.

6   Brush cookies with melted butter. Bake in the center of the oven until lightly golden, about 15 minutes. Let cool on the cookie sheets for 3 minutes, then transfer to wire racks to cool completely.

CHOCOLATE-NUT CRESCENTS

makes 36 cookies

A gooey filling of jam, chocolate, and nuts turns this cookie into a rich pastry.

COOKIE EXCHANGE TIP: Substitute cinnamon chips for the regular chips. Or, be creative and try one of the many other varieties of chips available, such as milk chocolate chips or white chocolate chips.

DOUGH

1 (8-OUNCE) PACKAGE CREAM CHEESE, AT ROOM TEMPERATURE, CUT INTO 2-INCH PIECES

1 CUP (2 STICKS) UNSALTED BUTTER, AT ROOM TEMPERATURE

2 LARGE EGG YOLKS

½ CUP SUGAR

2 TEASPOONS VANILLA EXTRACT

¼ TEASPOON SALT

2 CUPS ALL-PURPOSE FLOUR

FILLING

1 (12-OUNCE) JAR APRICOT JAM (ABOUT 1 CUP)

1 (12-OUNCE) PACKAGE SEMISWEET CHOCOLATE CHIPS (ABOUT 2 CUPS)

1 CUP FINELY CHOPPED WALNUTS OR PECANS, PREFERABLY TOASTED (SEE PAGE 38)

1 CUP SUGAR

3 TABLESPOONS GROUND CINNAMON

2 LARGE EGG WHITES, LIGHTLY BEATEN

1 Prepare the dough. In a large bowl, with an electric mixer, beat together the cream cheese and butter on medium speed until light, 2 to 3 minutes. Beat in the egg yolks, sugar, vanilla, and salt. On low speed, gradually beat in the flour just until mixed. The dough will be soft and sticky.

2 Divide the dough into 3 equal portions. Pat each portion into a thick disk and wrap separately in plastic wrap. Refrigerate until firm, at least 1 hour or up to 1 day.

3 Preheat the oven to 350°F. Lightly grease or spray cookie sheets.

4 Place 1 dough portion on a lightly floured pastry cloth or board, and roll out into a circle about 12 inches in diameter and ⅛ to ¼ inch thick. Gently spread one-third of the jam evenly over the dough. Sprinkle the jam evenly with one-third each of the chocolate chips and nuts. With a small, sharp knife or a pizza cutter, cut the dough into 12 equal wedges. Starting from the wide end, roll up each wedge toward the center, then curl the ends in slightly to form a crescent. Place the crescents on the prepared cookie sheets, spacing them about 1½ inches apart. Repeat with the 2 remaining dough portions.

5　In a small bowl, stir together the sugar and cinnamon. Brush the crescents with the egg white and sprinkle with the cinnamon sugar.

6　Bake in the center of the oven until firm to a light touch and golden, about 30 minutes. Let cool on the cookie sheets for 5 minutes, then transfer to wire racks to cool completely.

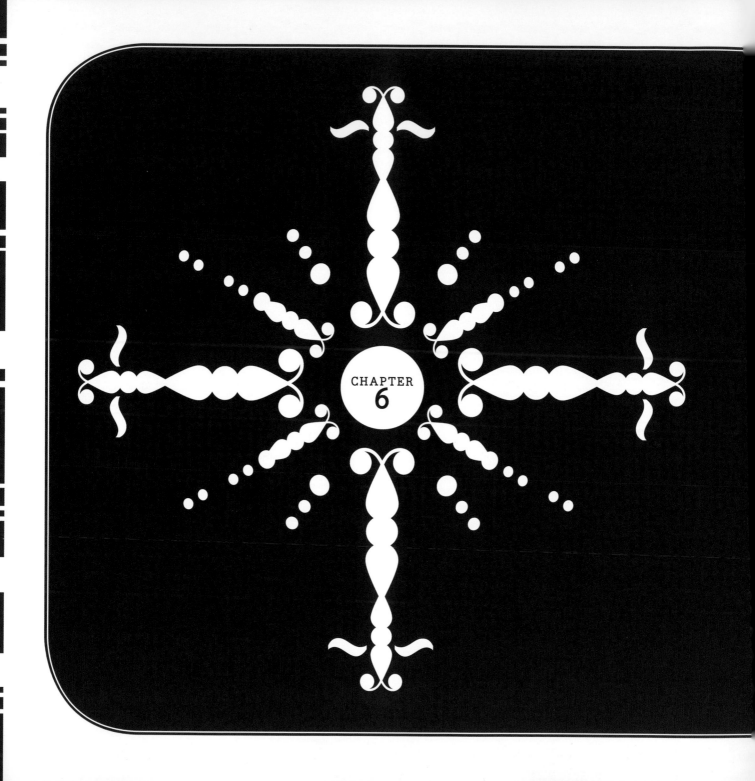

CHAPTER
6

MOLDED AND STAMPED COOKIES

Sometimes you want a cookie with a bit more elegance or pizzazz, a cookie that adds architectural interest to a plate of holiday treats. Stamped and molded cookies have been popular in Europe since medieval times.

For best results, use stamps specifically designed for cookies. We prefer ceramic cookie stamps (one popular brand is made of fired red clay) with handles.

Cookie molds were traditionally made of wood. Modern replicas are often made of resin (see Sources). Many modern molds are made of stoneware. Look for cookie molds in specialty foods shops and some crafts and hobby stores. Most molds are not meant to go into the oven; you shape the dough in the mold, then remove it before baking. Shortbread molds are an exception.

Making molded and stamped cookies is not difficult. For the best results, keep in mind:

1. The dough must be firm enough to be shaped or molded and to retain the design. If it is too sticky, refrigerate it until it is easier to handle. Or, if it is still sticky even when well chilled, add a little more flour. Also, use floured hands to handle the dough when pressing it into a mold.

2. The dough for molded cookies must be malleable enough so that when it is pressed into the mold, the design is transferred. If the dough is too dry or too cold, it will crack and the design will be lost.

3. Do not press dough into a mold too firmly or it will be difficult to remove it. Press lightly and evenly and then remove promptly.

4. Follow the manufacturer's directions when using molds. Some should be oiled, others floured. As you mold the cookies, dust the mold with flour or oil it as needed to keep the cookies from sticking. If you are having trouble with dough tearing or sticking even after following the manufacturer's directions, try flouring the mold instead of oiling it, or vice versa. Or, lightly oil and flour it.

5. Although cookie stamps come in all sorts of designs, we find that the simpler designs typically work best: holly, snowflakes, hearts, and so on.

FIVE-SPICE
SHORTBREAD

If you have a shortbread mold, use it in place of the baking pans to produce elegantly molded cookies.

COOKIE EXCHANGE TIP: This nontraditional shortbread with an Asian accent is sure to be a hit at any cookie exchange. Some people may be unfamiliar with five-spice powder, so bring along a jar to show them what it is.

1 CUP (2 STICKS) UNSALTED BUTTER, AT ROOM TEMPERATURE

½ CUP FIRMLY PACKED LIGHT BROWN SUGAR

1 TEASPOON VANILLA EXTRACT

2 CUPS ALL-PURPOSE FLOUR

¾ TEASPOON FIVE-SPICE POWDER

1 Preheat the oven to 325°F. Line two 8-inch square baking pans with heavy-duty aluminum foil, letting it slightly overhang 2 sides of the pan. (These "handles" will make it easier to lift the shortbread sheet from the pan.) Lightly grease or spray the aluminum foil.

2 In a large bowl, with an electric mixer, beat together the butter, sugar, and vanilla on medium speed until smooth and creamy, about 2 minutes. On low speed, gradually beat in the flour and five-spice powder just until mixed. The dough will be stiff.

3 Divide the dough in half. Press each half evenly into the bottom of a prepared pan. Smooth the top with lightly floured hands. Prick the top in several places with a fork. With a small, sharp knife, lightly score each shortbread sheet into 8 even wedges, being careful not to cut through the dough completely.

4 Bake on the top rack of the oven until firm and lightly golden, 20 to 25 minutes. Do not allow it to darken. Let cool completely in the pans on wire racks.

5 Retrace the scored lines in both pans with the knife. Grasp the foil on 2 sides and lift carefully to remove the shortbread sheet from each pan. Break gently into wedges.

CHOCOLATE-DIPPED
SHORTBREAD

makes **16** wedges

Chocolate chips melt faster than bar chocolate and firm up nicely as a coating, but you can also use a top-quality bittersweet chocolate. You will need 6 ounces; chop it before melting.

COOKIE EXCHANGE TIP: Play up the Scottish origin of these treats by decorating the tray with ribbons in red-and-green plaid.

1 CUP (2 STICKS) UNSALTED BUTTER, AT ROOM TEMPERATURE

⅔ CUP CONFECTIONERS' SUGAR

1¼ TEASPOONS VANILLA EXTRACT

2 CUPS ALL-PURPOSE FLOUR

½ CUP UNSWEETENED COCOA POWDER

1 CUP SEMISWEET CHOCOLATE CHIPS

1 Preheat the oven to 325°F. Line two 8-inch square baking pans with aluminum foil, letting it slightly overhang 2 sides of the pan. (These "handles" will make it easier to lift the shortbread sheet from the pan.)

2 In a large bowl, with an electric mixer, beat together the butter, sugar, and vanilla on medium speed until light and creamy, about 2 minutes. On low speed, gradually beat in the flour and cocoa just until mixed. The dough will be stiff.

3 Divide the dough in half. Press each half evenly into the bottom of a prepared pan. With a small, sharp knife, lightly score each shortbread sheet into 8 even wedges, being careful not to cut through the dough completely.

4 Bake on the top rack of the oven until firm to the touch, about 20 minutes. Let cool completely in the pans on wire racks.

continued . . .

. . . *continued*

5 Retrace the scored lines in both pans with the knife. Grasp the foil on 2 sides and lift carefully to remove the shortbread sheet from each pan. Break gently into wedges.

6 Place the chocolate chips in a microwave-safe bowl or in the top of a double boiler. Microwave at 80 percent power or heat over (not touching) barely simmering water, stirring occasionally, until melted and smooth (see page 67). Let cool slightly.

7 Dip one pointed end of each cooled shortbread wedge into the melted chocolate and set on a wire rack. Let stand until the chocolate sets.

CHRISTMAS MICE COOKIES

"'Twas the night before Christmas, when all through the house / Not a creature was stirring, not even a mouse . . ." Children enjoy helping to make these no-bake cookies, which are similar to a macaroon—somewhere between a cookie and a candy. Green (sour apple) candy whips, also called laces, make nice mouse tails. You can also use red or black licorice whips, or any color or flavor you like.

COOKIE EXCHANGE TIP: When arranging the platter, include a small wedge of cheese and position the mice so they are facing the cheese. You might even place one mouse on top of the cheese. These are very child-friendly cookies.

⅓ CUP SWEETENED CONDENSED MILK

GREEN FOOD COLORING

2 CUPS CONFECTIONERS' SUGAR

3 CUPS SWEETENED SHREDDED COCONUT

30 ALMOND SLICES

15 CURRANTS OR SMALL RED CANDIES

GREEN OR BLUE DECORATING PEN

GREEN (SOUR APPLE) WHIPS (LACES) OR OTHER CANDY WHIPS OF YOUR CHOICE, CUT INTO 6-INCH PIECES (15 PIECES TOTAL)

1   In a small cup, stir together the condensed milk and 2 or 3 drops food coloring, or enough to create a very pale green color. Make sure the food coloring is completely mixed through the milk.

2   In a food processor, combine the confectioners' sugar, coconut, and condensed milk mixture and process until all the ingredients are well combined and the coconut is finely minced, about 1 minute. Remove the blade from the food processor.

3   Scoop up a tablespoon of the coconut mixture, then gently push it out of the spoon with another spoon onto a work surface. Shape the mixture into a mouse, pinching a narrow nose on one end and a plump rear on the other. Using a spatula, transfer the mouse to a plate. Repeat until all the mice have been formed.

4   Place 2 almond slices on each mouse "head" to create ears, and put a currant or candy at the tip of the nose. Using the decorating pen, draw an eye on each mouse. Position a piece of candy whip for the tail on the plump rear, opposite the head. Cover the mice lightly with aluminum foil. Refrigerate until ready to serve.

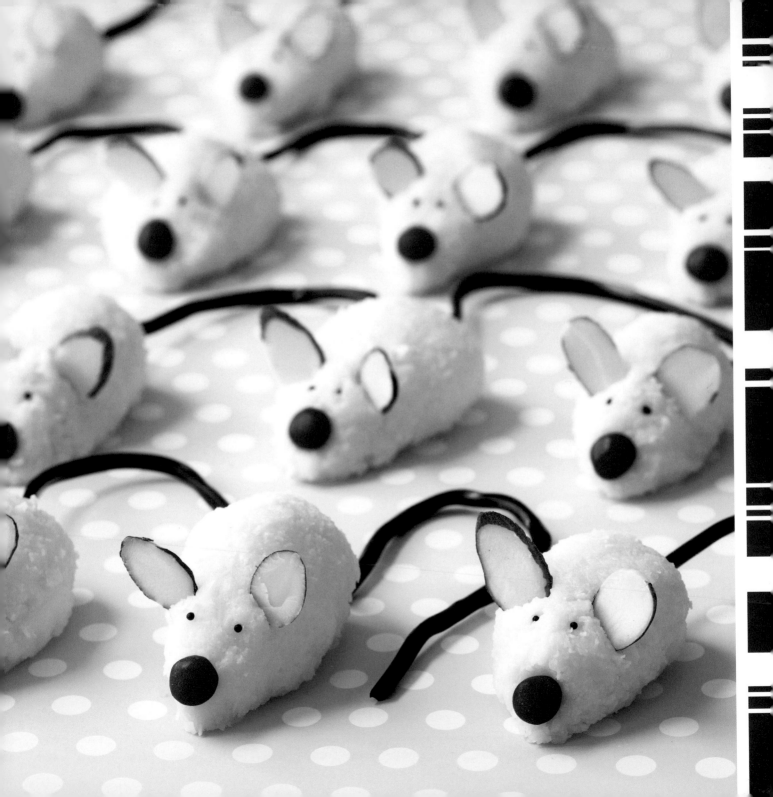

MOLDED
DUTCH SPICE COOKIES

In Holland, these spice-laced cookies, known as *speculaas*, are often molded in the shape of a windmill or of Santa, though many other designs are available as well. See Sources (page 240) for where you can purchase the molds.

COOKIE EXCHANGE TIP: The wooden mold used for making these Dutch cookies is attractive. Display it alongside the cookies.

2½ CUPS ALL-PURPOSE FLOUR

1 TEASPOON BAKING POWDER

½ TEASPOON SALT

2 TEASPOONS GROUND CINNAMON

½ TEASPOON GROUND NUTMEG

½ TEASPOON GROUND CLOVES

1 CUP (2 STICKS) UNSALTED BUTTER, AT ROOM TEMPERATURE

¾ CUP FIRMLY PACKED LIGHT BROWN SUGAR

1 TABLESPOON RUM, OR 2 TEASPOONS VANILLA EXTRACT

SLIVERED BLANCHED ALMONDS FOR TOPPING (OPTIONAL)

1 Preheat the oven to 350°F. Lightly grease or spray cookie sheets.

2 In a medium bowl, whisk together the flour, baking powder, salt, cinnamon, nutmeg, and cloves. Set aside.

3 In a large bowl, with an electric mixer, beat together the butter and sugar on medium speed until light, about 2 minutes. Beat in the rum. On low speed, gradually beat in the flour mixture just until mixed. The dough should be stiff, smooth, and pliable but not sticky.

4 Using a pastry brush, brush the *speculaas* mold(s) with flour. Press the dough into the molds, scraping off the excess, and unmold onto the prepared cookie sheets. (Or, place the dough on a lightly floured pastry cloth or board, and roll out ⅞ inch thick.) Using a cookie cutter in desired shape and size, cut out cookies. Using a spatula, transfer the cookies to the prepared cookie sheets, spacing them about 1½ inches apart. Gather the scraps, reroll, and cut out more cookies.

5 Top each cookie with several almond slivers, if desired, gently pressing the almonds into dough.

6 Bake in the center of the oven until the edges begin to turn golden, 9 to 11 minutes. Let cool on the cookie sheets for 1 to 2 minutes, then transfer to wire racks to cool completely.

ALMOND
CRESCENTS DIPPED IN WHITE CHOCOLATE

makes about
36
cookies

For an easier (and more traditional) recipe, omit the chocolate and dust the cookies with sifted confectioners' sugar while they are still warm.

COOKIE EXCHANGE TIP: Put a cloth Santa hat in the middle of the table (or platter). Line it with plastic wrap and arrange the cookies so they are spilling out of the hat, horn of plenty style.

1 CUP (2 STICKS) UNSALTED BUTTER, AT ROOM TEMPERATURE

¾ CUP SUGAR

1½ TEASPOONS VANILLA EXTRACT

2¼ CUPS ALL-PURPOSE FLOUR

1 CUP FINELY CHOPPED WALNUTS, HAZELNUTS, OR ALMONDS, PREFERABLY TOASTED (SEE PAGE 38)

1½ CUPS WHITE CHOCOLATE CHIPS

1   Preheat the oven to 350°F. Have ready nonstick cookie sheets.

2   In a large bowl, with an electric mixer, beat together the butter, sugar, and vanilla on medium speed until light, 2 to 3 minutes. On low speed, gradually beat in the flour just until mixed. Stir in the nuts. The dough will be stiff but pliable.

3   To shape each cookie, pinch off a walnut-size piece of dough. Roll each piece into a 3-inch rope. Place on the cookie sheets, spacing them about 1½ inches apart. Gently pull the ends of each cookie down to form a crescent shape.

4   Bake in the center of the oven until lightly golden on the bottom, 15 to 16 minutes. Let cool on the cookie sheets for 5 minutes, then transfer to wire racks to cool completely.

5   Place the chocolate chips in a microwave-safe bowl or in the top of a double boiler. Microwave at 50 percent power or heat over (not touching) barely simmering water, stirring occasionally, until melted and smooth (see page 67).

6   When the cookies are cool, dip both ends of each cookie into the melted chocolate. Return the cookies to the wire racks and let stand until the chocolate sets.

ALMOND TUILES

Plan on baking only 6 cookies at a time, since they must be molded while still hot. These cookies have an unusual shape reminiscent of European roof tiles, which is reflected in their name: *tuiles* means "tiles" in French.

COOKIE EXCHANGE TIP: *Tuiles* are fragile. Pack them in a single layer and cover lightly with aluminum foil for transport.

2 LARGE EGG WHITES, AT ROOM TEMPERATURE

½ CUP SUGAR

½ CUP GROUND BLANCHED ALMONDS

½ CUP ALL-PURPOSE FLOUR

4 TABLESPOONS (½ STICK) UNSALTED BUTTER, MELTED AND COOLED

1½ TEASPOONS ALMOND EXTRACT

½ TEASPOON VANILLA EXTRACT

½ CUP SLIVERED BLANCHED ALMONDS

1   Preheat the oven to 350°F. Lightly grease or spray a nonstick cookie sheet. Have ready a rolling pin or clean broom handle for shaping the cookies.

2   In a large bowl, with an electric mixer, beat together the egg whites and sugar on high speed until the egg whites are foamy and the sugar has been absorbed, about 2 minutes. On medium speed, beat in the ground almonds, flour, butter, and almond and vanilla extracts just until mixed. The dough will be soft and sticky.

3   Drop by heaping teaspoons onto the prepared cookie sheet, spacing them about 3 inches apart. Make 6 cookies at a time. Dip the tines of a fork in water and use to flatten the cookies gently, keeping a round shape about 3 inches in diameter. Sprinkle some slivered almonds on each cookie.

4   Bake in the center of the oven until just golden brown, 5 to 7 minutes. Let cool on the cookie sheet for about 30 seconds, then use a spatula to gently loosen the cookies from the pan. Working quickly, place each cookie on the rolling pin or broom handle, gently molding it into the curved shape. (If a cookie becomes too firm to shape, return it to the oven briefly; it will soften.) Carefully lift the cookies from the pin or handle and place on wire racks. Repeat with the remaining dough, regreasing or respraying the cookie sheet as necessary.

makes
80
cookies

MINI EGGNOG
MADELEINES

Light, delicate madeleines, made famous by Marcel Proust in *Remembrance of Things Past*, are baked in special pans, or plaques, with molds that give them a lovely scallop-shell shape. Thanks to the nutmeg, these madeleines taste like eggnog, making them a true holiday treat.

COOKIE EXCHANGE TIP: Madeleine pans come with oval molds in two sizes, regular or mini, and can be found in most well-stocked cookware stores. Here, a pan with mini molds is used. If you use a pan with larger molds, this recipe will yield 40 cookies—and you will be able to trade the cookies one for one at an exchange. For the larger molds, increase the baking time to 10 to 12 minutes.

½ CUP (1 STICK) UNSALTED BUTTER
2 LARGE EGGS
½ CUP SUGAR
¼ TEASPOON SALT
1 TEASPOON GROUND NUTMEG
1 CUP SIFTED CAKE FLOUR

1 In a small saucepan, melt the butter over low heat. Remove from the heat and let cool.

2 In a large bowl, with an electric mixer, beat together the eggs, sugar, salt, and nutmeg on high speed until light and tripled in volume, about 2 minutes. With a rubber spatula, gently fold in the flour, a few tablespoons at a time, just until incorporated. Then slowly and gently stir in the cooled butter just until combined.

3 Cover the bowl with plastic wrap and let the batter rest for 45 minutes at room temperature.

4 Preheat the oven to 375°F. Grease or spray a nonstick mini madeleine pan, being careful to reach all of the ridges or the madeleines will stick.

5 Spoon the batter into the prepared molds, filling each one three-fourths full.

6 Bake in the center of the oven until the cookies rise in the center and are very light brown on the edges, 6 to 8 minutes. They should spring back when lightly touched in the center. Do not overbake the cookies or they will be dry. Remove from the oven, invert the pan onto a wire rack, and tap lightly to release the cookies from the pan. Let cool completely. If you are baking madeleines in batches, let the pan cool completely and regrease it before baking the next batch.

SCANDINAVIAN
STAMP COOKIES

makes **40** cookies

A smooth, firm dough yields the sharpest design, so make sure the lemon zest is finely grated and the dough is cool. We often mince the zest in a food processor with the sugar to make sure it is fine enough. One medium lemon will yield about 2 teaspoons grated zest.

COOKIE EXCHANGE TIP: Serve these on a blue-and-white Scandinavian design plate or a tray lined with blue and white tiles.

1 CUP (2 STICKS) UNSALTED BUTTER, AT ROOM TEMPERATURE

½ CUP SUGAR

½ TEASPOON ALMOND EXTRACT

2 TEASPOONS FINELY GRATED LEMON ZEST

½ TEASPOON GROUND CARDAMOM

¼ TEASPOON SALT

2 CUPS ALL-PURPOSE FLOUR

1 In a large bowl, with an electric mixer, beat together the butter and sugar on medium speed until light, about 2 minutes. Beat in the almond extract, lemon zest (if you haven't minced it with the sugar), cardamom, and salt. On low speed, beat in the flour just until mixed. The dough will be stiff.

2 Gather the dough into a ball and wrap in plastic wrap. Refrigerate until firm, 30 to 40 minutes.

3 Preheat the oven to 325°F. Lightly grease or spray cookie sheets.

4 Pinch off pieces of the dough and roll between your palms into 1-inch balls. Place on the prepared cookie sheets, spacing them about 2 inches apart. Oil a cookie stamp and press down lightly on a ball to imprint the design. Repeat, oiling the stamp again after stamping every few cookies.

5 Bake in the center of the oven until no indentation remains when pressed very lightly, 12 to 15 minutes. Let cool on the cookie sheets for 2 minutes, then transfer to wire racks to cool completely.

KRINGLES

makes **30** cookies

This northern European knotted treat, known as *kringler* in Denmark and Norway and *kringla* in Sweden, is sometimes made with a yeast dough or puff pastry dough and is variously flavored with raisins, marzipan, and caraway. We use a simple cookie dough and lightly spice it with nutmeg and anise.

COOKIE EXCHANGE TIP: Sprinkle these pretzel-shaped cookies with coarse decorating sugar, to resemble the coarse salt on traditional pretzels.

1¾ CUPS ALL-PURPOSE FLOUR

½ TEASPOON BAKING POWDER

¼ TEASPOON BAKING SODA

½ CUP SOUR CREAM

4 TABLESPOONS (½ STICK) UNSALTED BUTTER, AT ROOM TEMPERATURE

½ CUP GRANULATED SUGAR

½ TEASPOON ANISE EXTRACT

¼ TEASPOON GROUND NUTMEG

1 LARGE EGG WHITE, LIGHTLY BEATEN

¼ CUP WHITE DECORATING SUGAR OR GRANULATED SUGAR

1   In a medium bowl, whisk together the flour, baking powder, and baking soda. Set aside.

2   In a large bowl, with an electric mixer, beat together the sour cream and butter on medium speed until smooth, about 1 minute. Beat in the granulated sugar, anise extract, and nutmeg until smooth. On low speed, beat in the flour mixture just until mixed. The dough will be medium-firm.

3   Gather the dough together, shape into a log about 10 inches long, and wrap in plastic wrap. Refrigerate until firm, about 2 hours.

4   Preheat the oven to 350°F. Lightly grease or spray nonstick cookie sheets.

5   Cut the dough into 10 equal portions. Roll each portion into a thin rope about 12 inches long. Cut each rope into 3 equal pieces each 4 inches long. Loop the ends of each piece around each other and then gently press the ends onto the circle, forming a pretzel shape. Place on the cookie sheets, spacing them about 1½ inches apart. Brush lightly with the egg white and sprinkle with the decorating sugar.

6   Bake in the center of the oven until firm to the touch and lightly golden on the bottom, 10 to 12 minutes. Let cool on the cookie sheets for 2 minutes, then transfer to wire racks to cool completely.

ITALIAN
TWISTED WREATH
COOKIES

makes 15 cookies

Serve these orange-flavored wreath cookies with espresso, milk, or orange-flavored tea.

COOKIE EXCHANGE TIP: Most ring-style cookies can be used as tree ornaments. For fun, decorate a small tabletop tree with these Italian-inspired wreaths.

1½ TABLESPOONS MILK OR ORANGE JUICE

⅓ CUP GRANULATED SUGAR

1 TEASPOON VANILLA EXTRACT

¼ CUP VEGETABLE SHORTENING

1½ CUPS SELF-RISING FLOUR

1 LARGE EGG

GLAZE

1 CUP CONFECTIONERS' SUGAR

2 TO 3 TABLESPOONS ORANGE JUICE

1 TEASPOON FINELY GRATED ORANGE ZEST

1 Preheat the oven to 350°F. Lightly grease or spray cookie sheets.

2 In a small, heavy saucepan, combine the milk and granulated sugar and simmer over low heat, stirring occasionally, until the sugar has dissolved, 3 to 4 minutes. Remove from the heat and stir in the vanilla. Let cool.

3 In a large bowl, with an electric mixer, beat the shortening on medium speed until smooth, about 2 minutes. On low speed, gradually beat in the flour just until mixed. Then, in a slow, steady stream, beat in the cooled milk mixture just until mixed. Beat in the egg. The dough will be stiff.

4 Gather the dough together and briefly knead on a lightly floured pastry cloth or board until smooth and pliable.

5 Pinch off teaspoons of the dough and roll each piece into a thin pencil shape about 5 inches long. When all of the pencil shapes have been formed (you should have 30), form a rope by attaching two "pencils" to each other at one end and then twisting them together to create a braided look. Form each braided pair into a circle and seal the ends together. Place on the prepared cookie sheets, spacing them about 2 inches apart.

6 Bake in the center of the oven until the cookies are firm and lightly golden, 16 to 18 minutes.

7 While the cookies are baking, prepare the glaze. In a medium bowl, whisk together the sugar, 2 tablespoons orange juice, and the orange zest until smooth. Add more orange juice, 1 teaspoon at a time, if needed to make the glaze spreadable.

8 When the cookies are ready, let cool on the cookie sheets for 2 minutes, then transfer to wire racks. While the cookies are hot, spread the glaze over them. Let stand until the cookies are completely cool and the glaze is dry and set.

BRANDY SNAPS

These toffee-colored, lacy English cookies date back to medieval times. They can be filled with sweetened whipped cream before serving. We like them plain, but you can tell the other cookie exchangers they can fill them.

COOKIE EXCHANGE TIP: These cookies will keep in an airtight container at room temperature for up to 10 days, so you can make them in advance. Be careful when you handle them, as they tend to be fragile.

4 TABLESPOONS (½ STICK) UNSALTED BUTTER

1 CUP FIRMLY PACKED LIGHT BROWN SUGAR

¼ CUP LIGHT CORN SYRUP

½ TEASPOON FRESH GRATED GINGER

1 CUP SIFTED ALL-PURPOSE FLOUR

½ TEASPOON BRANDY

1   Preheat the oven to 350°F. Grease or spray a nonstick cookie sheet. Have ready a wooden spoon with a long, round handle for shaping the cookies.

2   In a large, heavy saucepan, combine the butter, sugar, corn syrup, and ginger over medium heat and heat, stirring occasionally, until the butter and sugar have melted and all the ingredients are combined, about 2 minutes. Remove from the heat and stir in the flour and brandy. The batter will be medium thick.

3   Spoon a heaping teaspoon of the batter onto the prepared cookie sheet. Using the back of a spoon, spread the batter into a circle about 3 inches in diameter. Repeat, spacing the cookies at least 2 inches apart. Make only 4 cookies at a time, because they must be hot when they are rolled.

4   Bake in the center of the oven just until the cookies begin to firm up, 12 to 15 minutes. Remove from the oven. Working quickly, and using a spatula, lift a cookie from the cookie sheet and wrap it in a spiral around the handle of the wooden spoon. Let cool for 20 seconds, then slide the cookie off the spoon handle onto a wire rack to cool completely. (If the cookies harden too much to remove them from the cookie sheet and shape them, return the cookie sheet to the oven for about 1 minute. They will soften again.) Repeat with the remaining batter, regreasing or respraying the cookie sheet as necessary.

TURTLES

Inspired by the popular chocolate, caramel, and nut candies of the same name, these cookies use pecans to simulate the turtle's feet and tail.

COOKIE EXCHANGE TIP: Place each cookie in a holiday-themed paper cupcake liner, then set the filled liners on a festive platter.

1 CUP ALL-PURPOSE FLOUR

1 TEASPOON BAKING POWDER

¼ TEASPOON SALT

½ CUP (1 STICK) UNSALTED BUTTER, AT ROOM TEMPERATURE

1 CUP FIRMLY PACKED LIGHT BROWN SUGAR

1 LARGE EGG

½ TEASPOON VANILLA EXTRACT

90 PECAN PIECES

1 CUP SEMISWEET CHOCOLATE CHIPS

2 TABLESPOONS MILK

1 In a medium bowl, whisk together the flour, baking powder, and salt. Set aside.

2 In a large bowl, with an electric mixer, beat together the butter and sugar on medium speed until light, 2 to 3 minutes. Beat in the egg and vanilla. On low speed, gradually beat in the flour mixture just until mixed. The dough will be smooth and pliable.

3 Gather the dough into a ball and wrap in plastic wrap. Refrigerate until firm, about 1 hour.

4 Preheat the oven to 350°F. Have ready nonstick cookie sheets.

5 Drop the dough by teaspoons onto the cookie sheets, spacing them about 2 inches apart. Insert 3 pecan pieces into the bottom edge of each cookie, shaping a triangle with the nuts, to make the base of the turtle.

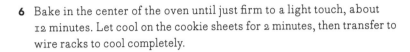

6 Bake in the center of the oven until just firm to a light touch, about 12 minutes. Let cool on the cookie sheets for 2 minutes, then transfer to wire racks to cool completely.

7 While the cookies are cooling, place the chocolate chips and milk in a microwave-safe bowl or in the top of a double boiler. Microwave at 80 percent power or heat over (not touching) barely simmering water, stirring occasionally, until melted and smooth (see page 67).

8 Using a pastry brush, evenly brush the tops of the cookies with the melted chocolate. Allow the cookies to cool completely. Let stand until the chocolate sets.

BOWKNOTS

makes **30** cookies

True to its name, the bowknot is a cookie shaped like a bow. These fried cookies are fun to make, but remember to slide them carefully, rather than drop them, into the hot oil, or you can cause splatters that can burn you. They are good warm or at room temperature, so sneak a taste before they cool and you pack them for the exchange.

COOKIE EXCHANGE TIP: Decorate the cookie-laden platter with bows in various colors.

6 LARGE EGG YOLKS

¼ CUP GRANULATED SUGAR

1 TABLESPOON UNSALTED BUTTER, MELTED

⅓ CUP HEAVY CREAM

¾ TEASPOON GROUND CARDAMOM

¼ TEASPOON SALT

2 CUPS ALL-PURPOSE FLOUR

VEGETABLE OIL FOR DEEP-FRYING

CONFECTIONERS' SUGAR FOR DUSTING

1   In a large bowl, with an electric mixer, beat the egg yolks on high speed until light, about 2 minutes. Gradually beat in the granulated sugar until smooth. On medium speed, beat in the butter, cream, cardamom, and salt. On low speed, beat in the flour. Then increase the speed to medium and beat just until the flour is fully incorporated. The dough will be soft.

2   Divide the dough in half. Pat each half into a thick disk and wrap separately in plastic wrap. Refrigerate until firm, at least 1 hour or up to overnight.

3   Place 1 dough disk on a lightly floured pastry cloth or board, and roll out ¼ inch thick. Cut the dough into strips 4 inches long by 1 inch wide. Cut a 3-inch-long lengthwise slit in the center of each strip. To "knot" each strip, pull one end of the strip through the slit. Repeat with the remaining dough disk.

4   Have ready a large tray lined with paper towels. Pour the oil to a depth of 1 inch in a heavy skillet and heat over medium-high heat to 375°F on a deep-frying thermometer. Slide 4 or 5 cookies into the hot oil and fry, turning as needed, until golden brown on both sides, 1 to 1½ minutes. Using a slotted spoon, transfer to the paper towels to drain. Repeat to fry the remaining cookies in the same way.

5   Sift the confectioners' sugar over the warm cookies, then let cool completely.

HONEY–PINE NUT CRESCENTS

It takes time to shape and top these cookies, but they are well worth the time and effort.

COOKIE EXCHANGE TIP: Pinecones and faux evergreen branches make a nice backdrop for these crescent-shaped cookies.

½ CUP (1 STICK) PLUS
2 TABLESPOONS UNSALTED BUTTER,
AT ROOM TEMPERATURE

½ CUP FIRMLY PACKED BROWN
SUGAR

2 LARGE EGG YOLKS

½ TEASPOON VANILLA EXTRACT

1 TABLESPOON FINELY GRATED
LEMON OR ORANGE ZEST

⅛ TEASPOON GROUND NUTMEG

4 TABLESPOONS HONEY

2 CUPS ALL-PURPOSE FLOUR

1 CUP CHOPPED PINE NUTS, PECANS,
OR HAZELNUTS, PREFERABLY
TOASTED (SEE PAGE 38)

1 Preheat the oven to 350°F. Lightly grease or spray cookie sheets.

2 In a large bowl, with an electric mixer, beat together the butter and sugar on medium speed until light, 2 to 3 minutes. Beat in the egg yolks, vanilla, lemon zest, nutmeg, and 2 tablespoons of the honey until smooth. On low speed, gradually beat in the flour just until mixed. The dough will be medium-firm. If it does not hold together, remove it from the bowl and knead on a lightly floured work surface for a few minutes until smooth.

3 Roll 1 tablespoon of the dough into a pencil shape about 2 inches long. Place on a prepared cookie sheet, and curve the ends to make a crescent shape. Repeat with the remaining dough, spacing the cookies about 1½ inches apart.

4 Heat the remaining 2 tablespoons honey in the microwave for a few seconds (or briefly on the stovetop) to thin it. Using a pastry brush, lightly brush the cookies with the honey, then gently press some nuts into the top of each cookie.

5 Bake in the center of the oven until just firm to the touch and beginning to turn golden, 8 to 10 minutes. Let cool on the cookie sheets for 3 minutes, then transfer to wire racks to cool completely.

CEREAL WREATH TREATS

makes about
20
wreaths

This easy no-bake cookie is an old holiday favorite. This version was shared with us by Diane Szczepaniak, whose mother, Irene, used to make them every Christmas.

COOKIE EXCHANGE TIP: These wreaths can be sticky, so slip a sheet of waxed paper between each layer for transport.

½ CUP (1 STICK) UNSALTED BUTTER

1 (10-OUNCE) PACKAGE REGULAR MARSHMALLOWS (ABOUT 40), OR 4 CUPS MINIATURE MARSHMALLOWS

GREEN FOOD COLORING

6 TO 7 CUPS CORNFLAKES

MINI RED CINNAMON CANDIES OR LARGE, RED ROUND SPRINKLES SUCH AS CAKE MATE'S DECORS

1 Butter cookie sheets.

2 In a large, heavy saucepan, melt the butter over low heat. Add the marshmallows and stir until completely melted. Stir in enough food coloring to create the desired shade of green. Remove from the heat. Stir in the cereal until evenly coated.

3 Drop by heaping spoonfuls (use about 3 tablespoons cereal mixture for each wreath) onto the prepared cookie sheets. With buttered or wet fingers, shape each mound into a ring to simulate a wreath. Decorate each wreath with the candies.

4 Let stand until firm, about 15 minutes.

CHAPTER
7

PRESSED AND PIPED COOKIES

There's no need to feel intimidated by cookie presses and pastry bags. All you need is a little practice to make you feel confident when you make cookies using these tools. Pressed, or spritz, cookie recipes deliver a bonus, too: Most of them yield at least four or five dozen cookies, making them good for exchanges. For the best results with pressed cookies, follow these simple guidelines:

1. Use cool, ungreased cookie sheets.

2. Press down firmly on the handle to shape the cookie, and then pull up the press before you release the handle.

3. If the dough is lifting up off the cookie sheet when you lift the press, try chilling the cookie sheets first.

4. The dough should be stiff but pliable. After testing a few cookies, you will know the correct consistency. If the cookies seem blurred or too soft, chill the dough for 15 minutes. If the dough is getting stuck in the press, it may be too stiff. Try adding a tablespoon of milk to it.

The piped cookie recipes here are based on meringue. Here are some tips on making a light meringue and piping it:

1. Have the egg whites at room temperature. You can use fresh egg whites or pasteurized egg whites from a carton.

2. Make sure your bowl and beaters are completely free of grease.

3. Avoid making meringues on humid days. The egg whites will not increase in volume as much as they should, and the finished cookies will absorb moisture from the air and lose their crispness.

4. Add the sugar slowly to allow the egg whites to absorb it gradually.

5. Use a rubber spatula or large spoon to spoon the meringue into the pastry bag. Do not fill the bag more than one-half full. Use your hand to smooth down the outside of the bag, pressing the filling down so there are no air bubbles.

6. As you pipe, apply pressure as consistently as possible to achieve uniform cookies, then lift the tip straight up without twisting it.

SPRITZ
CHRISTMAS TREES
AND WREATHS

These holiday trees and wreaths are festive. But if you don't have these disks on hand, press the dough into any shape you like and decorate as desired in seasonal colors.

COOKIE EXCHANGE TIP: Spritz cookies are pretty in themselves, so they don't need dressing up. Serve them on a plain red or green plate.

1 CUP (2 STICKS) UNSALTED BUTTER, AT ROOM TEMPERATURE

¾ CUP GRANULATED SUGAR

3 LARGE EGG YOLKS

½ TEASPOON VANILLA EXTRACT

½ TEASPOON ALMOND EXTRACT

2 OR 3 DROPS GREEN FOOD COLORING (OPTIONAL)

½ TEASPOON BAKING POWDER

2½ CUPS ALL-PURPOSE FLOUR

GREEN DECORATING SUGAR FOR SPRINKLING

RED SPRINKLES FOR DECORATING (OPTIONAL)

1 Preheat the oven to 350°F. Have ready ungreased cookie sheets.

2 In a large bowl, with an electric mixer, beat together the butter and granulated sugar on medium speed until light, 2 to 3 minutes. Beat in the egg yolks, vanilla and almond extracts, food coloring, and baking powder until smooth. On low speed, gradually beat in the flour just until mixed. The dough should be stiff, pliable, and only slightly sticky.

3 Divide the dough in half. Fill a cookie press fitted with a Christmas tree disk with half of the dough. (You may need to do this in two batches.) Press the cookies onto the cookie sheets, spacing them about 1½ inches apart. Press the second half of the dough through the press fitted with a wreath disk.

4 Sprinkle the cookies lightly with the green sugar. Decorate with the red sprinkles to look like treetop ornaments or berries.

5 Bake in the center of the oven until dry and set to the touch and just beginning to turn golden around the bottom edges, 10 to 12 minutes. Let cool on the cookie sheets for 2 minutes, then transfer to wire racks to finish cooling.

makes about **65** cookies

MOCHA TWEED **RIBBONS**

Grated chocolate and coffee crystals give these sophisticated, not-too-sweet cookies a speckled look that resembles tweed. To grate chocolate, break it into 2 or 3 pieces and grate on the fine (not extra-fine) holes of a grater.

COOKIE EXCHANGE TIP: For a fancier appearance, skip the confectioners' sugar and drizzle a little dark or white chocolate on the baked, cooled cookies.

1 CUP (2 STICKS) UNSALTED BUTTER, AT ROOM TEMPERATURE

½ CUP GRANULATED SUGAR

1 LARGE EGG YOLK

1 TEASPOON VANILLA EXTRACT

¼ TEASPOON SALT

½ CUP GRATED SEMISWEET CHOCOLATE (ABOUT 2 OUNCES)

1 TABLESPOON INSTANT COFFEE CRYSTALS

2 CUPS ALL-PURPOSE FLOUR

1 TO 2 TABLESPOONS MILK OR HEAVY CREAM, OR AS NEEDED

CONFECTIONERS' SUGAR FOR DUSTING

1   Preheat the oven to 350°F. Have ready ungreased cookie sheets.

2   In a large bowl, with an electric mixer, beat together the butter and granulated sugar on medium speed until light, about 2 minutes. Beat in the egg yolk, vanilla, and salt until smooth. On low speed, beat in the chocolate and coffee just until incorporated, then gradually beat in the flour just until mixed. Beat in enough milk to make a dough that is stiff, pliable, and only slightly sticky.

3   Fill a cookie press fitted with the ribbon disk with the dough. Press out 12-inch-long ribbons onto the cookie sheets. With a sharp paring knife, cut the ribbons into 2-inch lengths. Arrange the ribbons on the cookie sheets, spacing them about 1 inch apart.

4   Bake in the center of the oven until dry and set to the touch but not browned, 8 to 10 minutes. Let cool on the cookie sheets for 2 minutes, then transfer to wire racks to cool completely.

5   Sift the confectioners' sugar lightly over the cookies.

CHAI MERINGUES

makes about 48 cookies

Always mix and bake meringues on a clear, dry day for best results. On a humid day, they will absorb moisture and become sticky. Chai tea powder is found in well-stocked supermarkets and in specialty foods stores.

COOKIE EXCHANGE TIP: Place these pretty cookies in individual cupcake liners—silver or gold foil is nice—and arrange them on a doily-lined plate. To keep them fresh until you are ready to take them to the exchange, pack them in an airtight tin and store at room temperature.

6 EGG WHITES, AT ROOM TEMPERATURE

1½ CUPS SUGAR

⅛ TEASPOON SALT

1 TABLESPOON POWDERED CHAI MIX WITH NO SUGAR ADDED

1   Preheat the oven to 350°F. Line cookie sheets with aluminum foil or parchment paper.

2   In a large bowl, with an electric mixer, beat the egg whites on high speed until they form soft peaks. Sprinkle ¾ cup of the sugar over the egg whites and beat on high speed until incorporated. Sprinkle the salt, chai powder, and the remaining ¾ cup sugar over the egg whites and continue beating on high speed until stiff, glossy peaks form, 2 to 3 minutes.

3   Spoon the meringue into a pastry bag fitted with a ½-inch round tip, and pipe mounds about 1½ inches in diameter onto the prepared cookie sheets, spacing them about 1 inch apart. (Or, use 2 tablespoons to create mounds or drop by heaping teaspoons onto the prepared cookie sheets.)

4   Place in the top part and in the center of the oven. Turn off the oven, and do not open the oven door. Leave the meringues in the oven overnight. The next day, they should be firm to the touch. Carefully peel the foil away from the meringues.

SPICY CINNAMON
MERINGUES

makes about **36** cookies

These zesty cookies remind us a little of hot cinnamon candies.

COOKIE EXCHANGE TIP: Because some people don't like spicy food, you can play it safe by dividing the meringue in half and adding ¼ teaspoon black pepper to only half of it.

4 EGG WHITES, AT ROOM TEMPERATURE

⅛ TEASPOON SALT

1¼ CUPS SUGAR

1½ TEASPOONS GROUND CINNAMON

½ TEASPOON GROUND BLACK PEPPER

¼ TEASPOON GROUND CLOVES

¼ TEASPOON GROUND NUTMEG

1   Preheat the oven to 225°F. Line cookie sheets with aluminum foil or parchment paper.

2   In a large bowl, with an electric mixer, beat the egg whites and salt on high speed until foamy. Gradually beat in the sugar, a few tablespoons at a time. When all of the sugar has been added, continue beating until the meringue holds stiff, glossy peaks, about 3 minutes. Sprinkle the cinnamon, black pepper, cloves, and nutmeg over the beaten egg whites, then gently fold in with a rubber spatula.

3   Spoon the meringue into a pastry bag fitted with a ½-inch star tip, and pipe cookies 1½ inches in diameter onto the prepared cookie sheets, spacing them about 1 inch apart.

4   Bake in the center of the oven for 20 minutes. Turn off the oven, but do not open the oven door. Let the meringues stay in the closed oven until they are dry and crisp, several hours or up to overnight. Carefully peel the foil away from the meringues.

TWINKLING
LITTLE STARS

makes about
50
cookies

The glitter is optional, but it will give these pure white stars an eye-catching shimmer. If you're feeling ambitious, use a somewhat smaller closed or open star tip and pipe the meringue into five-pointed stars. Don't worry about being precise; freeform stars have more charm.

COOKIE EXCHANGE TIP: Line a pizza pan or similar shallow round pan with aluminum foil. Pour silver dragées into the pan, then pile the stars in the middle.

5 EGG WHITES, AT ROOM TEMPERATURE

⅛ TEASPOON SALT

1¼ CUPS GRANULATED SUGAR

1 TEASPOON CLEAR VANILLA EXTRACT

½ TEASPOON ALMOND EXTRACT

WHITE DECORATING SUGAR OR GRANULATED SUGAR FOR SPRINKLING

WHITE EDIBLE GLITTER FOR SPRINKLING (OPTIONAL)

1 Preheat the oven to 225°F. Line cookie sheets with aluminum foil or parchment paper.

2 In a large bowl, with an electric mixer, beat the egg whites and salt on high speed until foamy. Gradually beat in the granulated sugar, a few tablespoons at a time. When all of the sugar has been added, continue beating until the meringue holds stiff, glossy peaks, about 3 minutes. Beat in the vanilla and almond extracts just until combined.

3 Spoon the meringue into a pastry bag fitted with a large closed star tip, and pipe cookies just a bit larger than 1 inch in diameter onto the prepared cookie sheets, spacing them about 1 inch apart. Sprinkle the cookies with the decorating sugar and glitter, if desired.

4 Bake in the center of the oven for 30 minutes. Turn off the oven, but do not open the oven door. Let the meringues stay in the closed oven until they are dry and crisp, at least 4 hours and up to overnight. Carefully peel the foil away from the meringues.

SOURCES

AMERICAN SPOON
1668 CLARION AVENUE
PETOSKEY, MI 49770-0566
(800) 222-5886
WWW.AMERICANSPOON.COM

Jams and preserves (with and without added sugar), nuts, and dried tart Michigan cherries and blueberries.

CHOCOSPHERE.COM
PORTLAND, OREGON
(877) 992-4626
(503) 692-3323

Online store carries a large variety of chocolates, domestic and imported, including baking chocolates in bulk.

HOUSE ON THE HILL
650 WEST GRAND AVENUE
ELMHURST, IL 61026
(630) 279-4455
WWW.HOUSEONTHEHILL.NET

Individually hand-cast and hand-finished *speculaas* molds made in the United States. of a resin and wood composite, in a variety of designs. Most are replicas of antique carvings. Also sells baking and decorating supplies, including shortbread molds, shaped cake pans, edible decorator paints, marzipan, luster dust, food coloring, and springerle kits.

KING ARTHUR FLOUR
58 BILLINGS FARM ROAD
WHITE RIVER JUNCTION, VT 05001
(800) 827-6836
WWW.KINGARTHURFLOUR.COM

America's oldest flour company, founded in 1790. Sells a variety of regular and organic flours (including nut flours), bakeware, chocolate, yeast, and other baking ingredients.

KITCHEN COLLECTABLES
8901 J. STREET, SUITE 2
OMAHA, NE 68127
(888) 593-2436
WWW.KITCHENGIFTS.COM

More than 3,500 hand-crafted solid copper cookie cutters. Can create custom cookie cutters. Also sells decorating supplies, books, cookie jars, rolling pins, kitchen gadgets.

PENZEYS SPICES
PO BOX 26188
WAUWATOSA, WI 53226
(414) 760-7337
WWW.PENZEYS.COM

Extensive selection of spices and extracts at reasonable prices, including four different varieties of cinnamon; candied ginger chunks, slices, and nibs; and a double strength vanilla extract. Also has retail stores in twenty-four states. The Spice House (847-328-3711, www.thespicehouse.com) is also run by the Penzey family and sells most of the same spices.

INDEX

A

ALMONDS

ALMOND CRESCENTS DIPPED IN WHITE CHOCOLATE, 216

ALMOND TUILES, 217

AMARETTI, 104

CANDIED-FRUIT FLORENTINES, 118–19

CHOCOLATE-ORANGE COOKIES, 125

FINNISH ALMOND LOGS, 211

GERMAN STREUSEL COOKIES, 158–59

GINGER PFEFFERNUESSE, 57

GLACÉ CHERRY HOLIDAY SLICES, 166

HOLIDAY CINNAMON STARS, 161

ITALIAN TRICOLOR COOKIES, 140–41

LEBKUCHEN, 54–55

MACAROONS WITH ALMOND PASTE, 120

MOLASSES COOKIES WITH BUTTER-NUT TOPPING, 176–77

RASPBERRY LINZER SQUARES, 130–31

ROLLED COCONUT-STRAWBERRY COOKIES, 200–201

SAINT NICHOLAS COOKIES, 110–11

SOFT SANDWICH COOKIES, 185

SWEDISH THUMBPRINT COOKIES, 192–93

TOASTING, 38

TOFFEE SQUARES, 146

AMARETTI, 104

ANGELS, LARGE CINNAMON DOUGH, 84–87

ANIMAL SUGAR COOKIES, 40–42

APPLES

LARGE CINNAMON DOUGH ANGELS, 84–87

OLD-FASHIONED APPLE SQUARES, 137

APRICOTS

APRICOT BARS, 135–36

CHOCOLATE-NUT CRESCENTS, 202–3

ITALIAN TRICOLOR COOKIES, 140–41

KOLACKY, 189–90

B

BAKING TIPS

FOR BARS AND SQUARES, 127

FOR DROP COOKIES, 103

FOR FILLED COOKIES, 181

GENERAL, 30–31

FOR MOLDED AND STAMPED COOKIES, 205

FOR PRESSED AND PIPED COOKIES, 233

FOR ROLLED AND CUTOUT COOKIES, 149

FOR SLICE-AND-BAKE COOKIES, 165

BEAR PAWS, 191

BEVERAGES

CRANBERRY WASSAIL, 23

EGGNOG, 22

HOT CHOCOLATE WITH WHIPPED CREAM, 26

HOT MULLED WINE, 24

HOT WHITE CHOCOLATE WITH CINNAMON, 28

SPICED TEA PUNCH, 25

TIPS FOR, 21

BISCOTTI, PISTACHIO AND CRANBERRY, 171–72

BIZCOCHITOS, 163

BLACK AND WHITES, SMALL, 115–16

BOURBON

EGGNOG, 22

BOWKNOTS, 228–29

BRANDY

BRANDY SNAPS, 224

CRANBERRY WASSAIL, 23

BROWNIES

FUDGY BROWNIE BITS, 71

MARBLED CHOCOLATE–CREAM CHEESE BROWNIES, 45

BUTTER COOKIES, BASIC, 150

BUTTERCREAMS. SEE ICINGS AND FROSTINGS

BUTTERSCOTCH CHIPS

POINSETTIA COOKIES, 105

C

CANDY CANE COOKIES, 82

CEREAL

CEREAL WREATH TREATS, 231

CHOCOLATE RICE CEREAL ROCKING HORSES, 162

CRISPY CEREAL BARS WITH CHOCOLATE ON TOP, 145

CHAI MERINGUES, 237

CHECKERBOARD COOKIES, 174–75

CHERRIES

    CANDIED-FRUIT FLORENTINES, 118–19

    CHOCOLATE-CHERRY RIBBON COOKIES, 168–69

    GLACÉ CHERRY HOLIDAY SLICES, 166

    OATMEAL COOKIES WITH WHITE CHOCOLATE CHIPS AND DRIED CHERRIES, 37

    POINSETTIA COOKIES, 105

CHOCOLATE

    BEAR PAWS, 191

    CANDIED-FRUIT FLORENTINES, 118–19

    CHECKERBOARD COOKIES, 174–75

    CHOCOLATE BUTTERCREAM, 17

    CHOCOLATE-CHERRY RIBBON COOKIES, 168–69

    CHOCOLATE-DIPPED SHORTBREAD, 207–8

    CHOCOLATE-EDGED CHOCOLATE CHIP COOKIES, 36

    CHOCOLATE ICING, 115–16

    CHOCOLATE MINCEMEAT JUMBLES, 124

    CHOCOLATE-MINT BARS, 69–70

    CHOCOLATE-NUT CRESCENTS, 202–3

    CHOCOLATE-ORANGE COOKIES, 125

    CHOCOLATE PEANUT BUTTER CUPS, 197–98

    CHOCOLATE POURED FONDANT ICING, 15

    CHOCOLATE RICE CEREAL ROCKING HORSES, 162

CHOCOLATE SANDWICH COOKIES WITH MARSHMALLOW-MINT FILLING, 183–84

CHOCOLATE-TOPPED PECAN BARS, 144

CINNAMON CHIP–CHOCOLATE CHIP COOKIES, 74–75

CRISPY CEREAL BARS WITH CHOCOLATE ON TOP, 145

DARK CHOCOLATE COOKIES STUDDED WITH WHITE CHOCOLATE, 76

DEEP, DARK CHOCOLATE SANDWICH COOKIES, 62–64

DOUBLE-CHOCOLATE CHEWIES, 77

FATHER CHRISTMAS S'MORES, 46

FIVE-LAYER BARS, 133

FUDGY BROWNIE BITS, 71

HOT CHOCOLATE WITH WHIPPED CREAM, 26

ITALIAN TRICOLOR COOKIES, 140–41

KRIS KRINGLE COOKIES, 121

MALTED MILK CHOCOLATE COOKIES, 65

MARBLED CHOCOLATE–CREAM CHEESE BROWNIES, 45

MELTING, 67

MINI DEVIL'S FOOD CUPCAKES WITH WHITE CHOCOLATE FILLING, 72–73

MOCHA TWEED RIBBONS, 236

RED-NOSED RUDOLPH COOKIES, 99

SMALL BLACK AND WHITES, 115–16

TOFFEE SQUARES, 146

TURTLES, 226–27

TUXEDOED GINGERBREAD POLAR BEARS, 80–81

TYPES OF, 66

CHRISTMAS CUTOUT COOKIES, 152

CHRISTMAS MICE COOKIES, 212

CHRISTMAS TREES, SPRITZ, 234

CINNAMON

    CINNAMON CHIP–CHOCOLATE CHIP COOKIES, 74–75

    CINNAMON-NUT HORNS, 199

    HOLIDAY CINNAMON STARS, 161

    LARGE CINNAMON DOUGH ANGELS, 84–87

    SPICY CINNAMON MERINGUES, 238

COCOA POWDER, 66

COCONUT

    FIVE-LAYER BARS, 133

    LEMON BARS WITH A COCONUT CRUST, 138–39

    POINSETTIA COOKIES, 105

    ROLLED COCONUT-STRAWBERRY COOKIES, 200–1

    TOASTING, 38

COFFEE

    MOCHA TWEED RIBBONS, 236

COOKIE EXCHANGES

    MENUS FOR, 21

    PLANNING AND HOSTING, 11

    "RULES" FOR, 12–13

    THEMES FOR, 20–21

COOKIES. *SEE ALSO INDIVIDUAL RECIPES*

    DECORATING, 13–19

    PACKAGING, 20

    PRESENTATION OF, 20

    STORING BAKED, 31

    STORING DOUGH, 31

CRANBERRIES

CRANBERRY WASSAIL, 23

PISTACHIO AND CRANBERRY BISCOTTI, 171–72

CREAM CHEESE

CHOCOLATE-NUT CRESCENTS, 202–3

CREAM CHEESE SUGAR COOKIES WITH DULCE DE LECHE, 154–56

KOLACKY, 189–90

MARBLED CHOCOLATE–CREAM CHEESE BROWNIES, 45

ROLLED COCONUT-STRAWBERRY COOKIES, 200–1

RUM-RAISIN FROSTING, 58

CROATIAN JAM-FILLED WALNUT MERINGUE BARS, 132

CUPCAKES

MINI DEVIL'S FOOD CUPCAKES WITH WHITE CHOCOLATE FILLING, 72–73

MINI GINGERBREAD CUPCAKES WITH RUM-RAISIN FROSTING, 58

CURRANTS

CINNAMON-NUT HORNS, 199

TWO-BITE OATMEAL SANDWICH COOKIES WITH NUTELLA FILLING, 186–87

CUSTARD BARS, GREEK, 142–43

CUTOUT COOKIES, CHRISTMAS, 152

D

DATE-FILLED BARS, 128–29

DEVIL'S FOOD CUPCAKES, MINI, WITH WHITE CHOCOLATE FILLING, 72–73

DULCE DE LECHE, 155–56

DUSTS, 19

DUTCH SPICE COOKIES, MOLDED, 214

E

EGGNOG, 22

EGGNOG SNICKERDOODLES, 39

MINI EGGNOG MADELEINES, 218–19

F

FATHER CHRISTMAS S'MORES, 46

FIG JAM, PINE-NUT THUMBPRINT COOKIES WITH, 194

FINNISH ALMOND LOGS, 211

FIVE-LAYER BARS, 133

FIVE-SPICE SHORTBREAD, 206

FLORENTINES, CANDIED-FRUIT, 118–19

FONDANT ICING, POURED, 15

FOOD COLORINGS, 18

FROSTINGS. SEE ICINGS AND FROSTINGS

FRUIT, CANDIED

CANDIED-FRUIT FLORENTINES, 118–19

GLACÉ CHERRY HOLIDAY SLICES, 166

SAINT NICOLAS COOKIES, 110–11

FUDGY BROWNIE BITS, 71

G

GERMAN STREUSEL COOKIES, 158–59

GINGER

BASIC GINGERBREAD, 50–51

DOUBLE GINGERSNAPS, 56

GINGER PFEFFERNUESSE, 57

GINGER SHORTBREAD, 210

MINI GINGERBREAD CUPCAKES WITH RUM-RAISIN FROSTING, 58

OLD SALEM MOLASSES GINGER COOKIES, 52

RED-NOSED RUDOLPH COOKIES, 99

TUXEDOED GINGERBREAD POLAR BEARS, 80–81

GRAHAM CRACKERS

CHOCOLATE-MINT BARS, 69–70

FATHER CHRISTMAS S'MORES, 46

FIVE-LAYER BARS, 133

SANTA GRAHAMS, 151

GREEK CUSTARD BARS, 142–43

GREEN TEA–LEMON WAFERS, 117

H

HAZELNUTS

ALMOND CRESCENTS DIPPED IN WHITE CHOCOLATE, 216

CHOCOLATE-ORANGE COOKIES, 125

CINNAMON-NUT HORNS, 199

KRIS KRINGLE COOKIES, 121

LEBKUCHEN, 54–55

SAINT NICHOLAS COOKIES, 110–11

TOASTING, 38

HOLIDAY CINNAMON STARS, 161

HONEY–PINE NUT CRESCENTS, 230

I

ICINGS AND FROSTINGS

CHOCOLATE BUTTERCREAM, 17

CHOCOLATE ICING, 115–16

CHOCOLATE POURED FONDANT ICING, 15

EASY VANILLA ICING, 16

LEMON ICING, 111, 112–13

PIPING, 13

POURED FONDANT ICING, 15

ROYAL ICING, 14

RUM-RAISIN FROSTING, 58

TIPS FOR, 13

VANILLA BUTTERCREAM, 17

VANILLA ICING, 115–16

ITALIAN TRICOLOR COOKIES, 140–41

ITALIAN TWISTED WREATH COOKIES, 222–23

K

KOLACKY, 189–90

KRINGLES, 221

KRIS KRINGLE COOKIES, 121

L

LACE COOKIES, 109

LEBKUCHEN, 54–55

LEMONS

GREEN TEA–LEMON WAFERS, 117

LEMON BARS WITH A COCONUT CRUST, 138–39

LEMON-ICED COOKIES, 112–13

LEMON ICING, 111, 112–13

MINCEMEAT AND LEMON COOKIES, 178

LIME-PISTACHIO THINS, 179

LINGONBERRY JAM OR JELLY

SWEDISH THUMBPRINT COOKIES, 192–93

LINZER SQUARES, RASPBERRY, 130–31

M

MACADAMIA NUTS

DOUBLE-CHOCOLATE CHEWIES, 77

TOASTING, 38

MACAROONS WITH ALMOND PASTE, 120

MADELEINES, MINI EGGNOG, 218–19

MALTED MILK CHOCOLATE COOKIES, 65

M&M'S

RED-NOSED RUDOLPH COOKIES, 99

XMAS M&M'S COOKIES, 43

MARBLED CHOCOLATE–CREAM CHEESE BROWNIES, 45

MARSHMALLOWS

CEREAL WREATH TREATS, 231

CHOCOLATE RICE CEREAL ROCKING HORSES, 162

CHOCOLATE SANDWICH COOKIES WITH MARSHMALLOW-MINT FILLING, 183–84

CRISPY CEREAL BARS WITH CHOCOLATE ON TOP, 145

FATHER CHRISTMAS S'MORES, 46

HOMEMADE MARSHMALLOWS, 29

MENUS, 21

MERINGUES

CHAI MERINGUES, 237

CROATIAN JAM-FILLED WALNUT MERINGUE BARS, 132

MERINGUE SNOWFLAKES, 93–94

MINT MERINGUE WREATHS, 91

SPICY CINNAMON MERINGUES, 238

TWINKLING LITTLE STARS, 239

MICE COOKIES, CHRISTMAS, 212

MINCEMEAT

CHOCOLATE MINCEMEAT JUMBLES, 124

MINCEMEAT AND LEMON COOKIES, 178

MINT

CHOCOLATE-MINT BARS, 69–70

CHOCOLATE SANDWICH COOKIES WITH MARSHMALLOW-MINT FILLING, 183–84

MINT MERINGUE WREATHS, 91

MOCHA TWEED RIBBONS, 236

MOLASSES COOKIES WITH BUTTER-NUT TOPPING, 176–77

MOLDS, 205

N

NUTELLA FILLING, TWO-BITE OATMEAL SANDWICH COOKIES WITH, 186–87

NUTS, TOASTING, 38. SEE ALSO INDIVIDUAL NUTS

O

OATS

DATE-FILLED BARS, 128–29

LACE COOKIES, 109

OATMEAL BRICKLE NUGGETS, 122

OATMEAL COOKIES WITH WHITE CHOCOLATE CHIPS AND DRIED CHERRIES, 37

TWO-BITE OATMEAL SANDWICH COOKIES WITH NUTELLA FILLING, 186–87

XMAS M&M'S COOKIES, 43

ORANGES

CHOCOLATE-ORANGE COOKIES, 125

ORANGE-SCENTED SNOWBALLS, 108

ORNAMENTS

    CANDY CANE COOKIES, 82

    HAND-PAINTED XMAS COOKIE RINGS, 89–90

    LARGE CINNAMON DOUGH ANGELS, 84–87

    MERINGUE SNOWFLAKES, 93–94

    MINT MERINGUE WREATHS, 91

    RED-NOSED RUDOLPH COOKIES, 99

    STAINED-GLASS ORNAMENTS, 97–98

    SUGAR PRETZELS, 95

    TIPS FOR, 79

    TUXEDOED GINGERBREAD POLAR BEARS, 80–81

P

PEANUT BUTTER

    CHOCOLATE PEANUT BUTTER CUPS, 197–98

    CRISPY CEREAL BARS WITH CHOCOLATE ON TOP, 145

    STAMPED PEANUT BUTTER COOKIES, 44

PECANS

    BEAR PAWS, 191

    CHOCOLATE-EDGED CHOCOLATE CHIP COOKIES, 36

    CHOCOLATE-NUT CRESCENTS, 202–3

    CHOCOLATE-TOPPED PECAN BARS, 144

    CINNAMON-NUT HORNS, 199

    DARK CHOCOLATE COOKIES STUDDED WITH WHITE CHOCOLATE, 76

    DOUBLE-CHOCOLATE CHEWIES, 77

    FIVE-LAYER BARS, 133

    FUDGY BROWNIE BITS, 71

LACE COOKIES, 109

MINCEMEAT AND LEMON COOKIES, 178

OLD-FASHIONED APPLE SQUARES, 137

SAINT NICHOLAS COOKIES, 110–11

SAND TARTS, 160

SEEDY, NUTTY LITTLE SLICES, 173

TOASTING, 38

TURTLES, 226–27

PFEFFERNUESSE, GINGER, 57

PHYLLO DOUGH

    GREEK CUSTARD BARS, 142–43

PINE NUTS

    HONEY–PINE NUT CRESCENTS, 230

    PINE-NUT THUMBPRINT COOKIES WITH FIG JAM, 194

    SEEDY, NUTTY LITTLE SLICES, 173

PIPING, 13

PISTACHIOS

    GLACÉ CHERRY HOLIDAY SLICES, 166

    LIME-PISTACHIO THINS, 179

    PISTACHIO AND CRANBERRY BISCOTTI, 171–72

POINSETTIA COOKIES, 105

POLAR BEARS, TUXEDOED GINGERBREAD, 80–81

PRETZELS

    RED-NOSED RUDOLPH COOKIES, 99

    SUGAR PRETZELS, 95

PRUNES

    KOLACKY, 189–90

PUMPKIN SEEDS

    SEEDY, NUTTY LITTLE SLICES, 173

PUNCH, SPICED TEA, 25

R

RAISINS

    OLD-FASHIONED APPLE SQUARES, 137

    RUM-RAISIN FROSTING, 58

RASPBERRY JAM

    BEAR PAWS, 191

    CINNAMON-NUT HORNS, 199

    RASPBERRY LINZER SQUARES, 130–31

    SOFT SANDWICH COOKIES, 185

RED-NOSED RUDOLPH COOKIES, 99

ROCKING HORSES, CHOCOLATE RICE CEREAL, 162

ROYAL ICING, 14

RUDOLPH COOKIES, RED-NOSED, 99

RUM

    EGGNOG, 22

    RUM-RAISIN FROSTING, 58

RUSSIAN WALNUT TEA CAKES, 106

S

SAINT NICHOLAS COOKIES, 110–11

SAND TARTS, 160

SANTA GRAHAMS, 151

SCANDINAVIAN STAMP COOKIES, 220

SESAME SEEDS

    SEEDY, NUTTY LITTLE SLICES, 173

SHORTBREAD

    CHOCOLATE-DIPPED SHORTBREAD, 207–8

    FIVE-SPICE SHORTBREAD, 206

    GINGER SHORTBREAD, 210

S'MORES, FATHER CHRISTMAS, 46

SNICKERDOODLES, EGGNOG, 39

SNOWBALLS, ORANGE-SCENTED, 108

SNOWFLAKES, MERINGUE, 93–94

SPRINKLES, 19

SPRITZ CHRISTMAS TREES AND WREATHS, 234

STAINED-GLASS ORNAMENTS, 97–98

STAMPS, 205

STARS

HOLIDAY CINNAMON STARS, 161

TWINKLING LITTLE STARS, 239

STENCILING, 18

STRAWBERRY-COCONUT COOKIES, ROLLED, 200–201

STREUSEL COOKIES, GERMAN, 158–59

SUGARS, DECORATING, 18–19

SUNFLOWER SEEDS

SEEDY, NUTTY LITTLE SLICES, 173

SWEDISH THUMBPRINT COOKIES, 192–93

T

TEA

CHAI MERINGUES, 237

GREEN TEA–LEMON WAFERS, 117

SPICED TEA PUNCH, 25

TEA CAKES, RUSSIAN WALNUT, 106

THEMES, 20–21

THUMBPRINT COOKIES

PINE-NUT THUMBPRINT COOKIES WITH FIG JAM, 194

SWEDISH THUMBPRINT COOKIES, 192–93

TOFFEE

OATMEAL BRICKLE NUGGETS, 122

TOFFEE SQUARES, 146

TUILES, ALMOND, 217

TURTLES, 226–27

TUXEDOED GINGERBREAD POLAR BEARS, 80–81

TWINKLING LITTLE STARS, 239

TWO-BITE OATMEAL SANDWICH COOKIES WITH NUTELLA FILLING, 186–87

V

VANILLA

EASY VANILLA ICING, 16

SMALL BLACK AND WHITES, 115–16

VANILLA BUTTERCREAM, 17

VANILLA ICING, 115–16

VANILLA SANDWICH COOKIES, 182

W

WALNUTS

ALMOND CRESCENTS DIPPED IN WHITE CHOCOLATE, 216

BEAR PAWS, 191

CHOCOLATE-EDGED CHOCOLATE CHIP COOKIES, 36

CHOCOLATE-NUT CRESCENTS, 202–3

CHOCOLATE-ORANGE COOKIES, 125

CINNAMON-NUT HORNS, 199

CROATIAN JAM-FILLED WALNUT MERINGUE BARS, 132

DARK CHOCOLATE COOKIES STUDDED WITH WHITE CHOCOLATE, 76

DOUBLE-CHOCOLATE CHEWIES, 77

KRIS KRINGLE COOKIES, 121

LACE COOKIES, 109

MINCEMEAT AND LEMON COOKIES, 178

MOLASSES COOKIES WITH BUTTER-NUT TOPPING, 176–77

OLD-FASHIONED APPLE SQUARES, 137

ROLLED COCONUT-STRAWBERRY COOKIES, 200–201

RUSSIAN WALNUT TEA CAKES, 106

SAINT NICHOLAS COOKIES, 110–11

SWEDISH THUMBPRINT COOKIES, 192–93

TOASTING, 38

WASSAIL, CRANBERRY, 23

WHIPPED CREAM, 26

WHITE CHOCOLATE, 66

ALMOND CRESCENTS DIPPED IN WHITE CHOCOLATE, 216

DARK CHOCOLATE COOKIES STUDDED WITH WHITE CHOCOLATE, 76

HOT WHITE CHOCOLATE WITH CINNAMON, 28

MELTING, 67

MINI DEVIL'S FOOD CUPCAKES WITH WHITE CHOCOLATE FILLING, 72–73

OATMEAL COOKIES WITH WHITE CHOCOLATE CHIPS AND DRIED CHERRIES, 37

WINE, HOT MULLED, 24

WREATHS

CEREAL WREATH TREATS, 231

ITALIAN TWISTED WREATH COOKIES, 222–23

MINT MERINGUE WREATHS, 91

SPRITZ WREATHS, 234

X

XMAS M&M'S COOKIES, 43

TABLE OF EQUIVALENTS

SOLID MEASURES
OUNCES AND POUNDS,
WITH ROUNDED METRIC CONVERSIONS

1 ounce = 28 grams

2 ounces = 56 grams

4 ounces = 112 grams

8 ounces = 225 grams

16 ounces, or 1 pound = 45 grams

24 ounces, or 1½ pounds = 675 grams

32 ounces, or 2 pounds = 900 grams

LIQUID MEASURES,
WITH METRIC CONVERSIONS
BRITISH STANDARDS

1 teaspoon = 5 milliliters

1 tablespoon = 14 milliliters

4 tablespoons = 56 milliliters

¼ pint = 140 milliliters

½ pint = 280 milliliters

1 pint = 570 milliliters

LIQUID MEASURES,
WITH ROUNDED METRIC CONVERSIONS
UNITED STATES STANDARDS

1 teaspoon = 5 milliliters

2 teaspoons, or ¼ fluid ounce = 10 milliliters

1 tablespoon, or ½ fluid ounce = 14 milliliters

2 tablespoons (⅛ cup), or 1 fluid ounce = 28 milliliters

¼ cup, or 2 fluid ounces = 56 milliliters

½ cup, or 4 fluid ounces = 110 milliliters

1 cup, or 8 fluid ounces = 225 milliliters

2½ cups, or 1 pint, or 16 fluid ounces = 450 milliliters